Introduction

What a dull place our world would be without animals! The variety of animals is so vast and each has such unique characteristics. As quilters, we love to celebrate the variety, colors and patterns suggested to us by our partners on this earth. I have taken just a few—from the barnyards, jungles, woodlands, sky and ocean—to use for this collection of quilts and quilted projects. From turtles and chickens to elephants and whales, there are projects for the home and for gift-giving.

I have included sewing tips along the way and have also provided some design tips—ideas for using the techniques or appliqués in other ways. I hope you find them useful!

Meet the Designer

Chris Malone has been sewing and crafting most of her life. As an accomplished sewist, quilter and designer, she has had hundreds of designs published in sewing and quilting publications and has authored several books of her own.

She is a regular contributor to *Quilter's World* magazine and to Annie's quilting and sewing book titles. Chris's whimsical style has been a favorite of many quilters and sewists, and is easily recognizable at a glance.

Chris resides in the diverse and beautiful Willamette Valley of Oregon.

Table of Contents

General Instructions

You probably already have most of the supplies needed for these projects. Even so, here are a few tips on materials and tools, general assembly instructions and finishing tips that you may find helpful.

Basic Tools & Supplies

- Scissors for paper and fabric
- Rotary cutter and mat
- Nonslip quilting rulers
- Nonpermanent fabric-marking tools
- Template material
- Sewing machine
- Walking or even-feed foot (optional)
- Hand-sewing needles
- Straight pins and pincushion
- Curved safety pins for basting
- Seam ripper
- Steam/dry iron and ironing surface

Fabric & Thread

For best results, use only good-quality 100 percent cotton fabric and quality thread. Your time is worth it. If you are prewashing, do so with ALL of the fabrics being used. Generally, prewashing is not required in quilting.

Fusible Web With Paper Release

There are a lot of appliquéd projects in this book, and many have been made using fusible web with paper release and machine blanket-stitched edges. Always follow the manufacturer's directions for fusing times as brands do vary. Of course, if you prefer to hand-appliqué or use other methods of machine appliqué, feel free to do so.

Batting

Almost any low- or mid-loft batting will work for these projects. For items that will be subjected to heat, such as coasters, using one or two layers of cotton batting along with needle-punched insulated batting is suggested.

A needle-punched insulated batting reflects heat and cold back to the source. This breathable material has deep fibers that prevent conduction and a reflective metalized film that prevents radiant energy from passing through. Do not add this batting in anything you will be using in the microwave.

Template Material

Template material can be as simple as a clean and recycled cereal box or cardstock. If you will need to use the same pattern for many tracings, the translucent plastic material available at quilt shops is easy to use and will last indefinitely.

Walking or Even-Feed Foot

A walking or even-feed foot attachment for your sewing machine is a very helpful tool when sewing layers, and it is useful for simple quilting patterns as well. This foot feeds the upper and lower layers of fabric through the machine at the same rate.

Pinking Shears

Since a lot of the projects have curved pieces that are sewn and turned, consider adding a pair of pinking shears to your toolbox if you don't already have them. If you cut around curved seams with the pinking shears, you eliminate the need to clip the curves with straight-edge scissors, saving some time and effort. Pinking shears can also be used to control fraying on seam edges.

General Assembly Instructions

Read all instructions carefully before beginning each project.

All seams are ¼" unless otherwise directed.

The measurements given for each project include the outer seam allowance.

Press each seam as you sew.

Appliqué

Many of the projects in this book are made using a fusible web with paper release and a machine blanket stitch. Refer to Raw-Edge Fusible Appliqué on page 5 for specifics. Other appliqué methods may be substituted if desired. All of the appliqué patterns are reversed so they will face the correct direction when fused to the background. When appliqués overlap, slip one edge under the other ¼" before fusing.

Sometimes, appliqué fabric is so light colored or thin that the background fabric shows through excessively. You can correct this transparency problem by fusing a piece of lightweight interfacing to the wrong side of the fabric and then applying the fusible web with the marked pattern to the interfacing side. Cut out and use in the same way.

When arranging appliqué pieces on the background, use a straight pin to drag the pieces in place.

If the appliqué is large and you want to reduce the stiffness, cut out the center of the fusible web shape after drawing the pattern onto the paper side of the web. Just leave a margin of ¼"–½" inside the pattern line. This gives a border of adhesive to fuse to the background and leaves the center soft and easy to quilt.

If your fabric puckers during the machine stitching, use a light- to medium weight stabilizer behind the appliqué. Some of the project instructions call for a piece of batting to be basted to the wrong side of the fabric background piece before appliquéing; this batting will act as a stabilizer.

If using a machine blanket stitch for an edge finisher, practice going around curves. You need to move the fabric as often as necessary to keep the stitch going into the appliqué as perpendicular as possible to the edge. When you get to corners, place a stitch at the point before pivoting to stitch the next side. Be sure the needle is in the down position when you pivot the fabric. ●

Raw-Edge Fusible Appliqué

One of the easiest ways to appliqué is the raw-edge fusible-web method. Paper-backed fusible web individual pieces are fused to the wrong side of specified fabrics, cut out and then fused together in a motif or individually to a foundation fabric, where they are machine-stitched in place.

Choosing Appliqué Fabrics

Depending on the appliqué, you may want to consider using batiks. Batik is a much tighter weave and, because of the manufacturing process, does not fray. If you are thinking about using regular quilting cottons, be sure to stitch your raw-edge appliqués with blanket/buttonhole stitches instead of a straight stitch.

Cutting Appliqué Pieces

1. Fusible appliqué shapes should be reversed for this technique.

2. Trace the appliqué shapes onto the paper side of paper-backed fusible web. Leave at least ¼" between shapes. Cut out shapes leaving a margin around traced lines. **Note:** *If doing several identical appliqués, trace reversed shapes onto template material to make reusable templates for tracing shapes onto the fusible web.*

3. Follow manufacturer's instructions and fuse shapes to wrong side of fabric as indicated on pattern for color and number to cut.

4. Cut out appliqué shapes on traced lines. Remove paper backing from shapes.

5. Again following fusible web manufacturer's instructions, arrange and fuse pieces to quilt referring to quilt pattern. Or fuse together shapes on top of an appliqué ironing mat to make an appliqué motif that can then be fused to the quilt.

Stitching Appliqué Edges

Machine-stitch appliqué edges to secure the appliqués in place and help finish the raw edges with matching or invisible thread (Photo 1). **Note:** *To show stitching, all samples have been stitched with contrasting thread.*

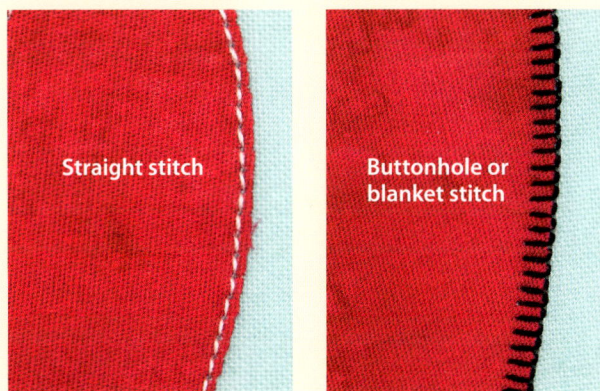

Straight stitch

Buttonhole or blanket stitch

Photo 1

Invisible thread can be used to stitch appliqués down when using the blanket or straight stitches. Do not use it for the satin stitch. Definitely practice with invisible thread before using it on your quilt; it can sometimes be difficult to work with.

A short, narrow buttonhole or blanket stitch is most commonly used (Photo 2). Your machine manual may also refer to this as an appliqué stitch. Be sure to stitch next to the appliqué edge with the stitch catching the appliqué.

Photo 2

Practice turning inside and outside corners on scrap fabric before stitching appliqué pieces. Learn how your machine stitches so that you can make the pivot points smooth.

1. To stitch outer corners, stitch to the edge of the corner and stop with needle in the fabric at the corner point. Pivot to the next side of the corner and continue to sew (Photo 3). You will get a box on an outside corner.

Photo 3

2. To stitch inner corners, pivot at the inner point with needle in fabric (Photo 4). You will see a Y shape in the corner.

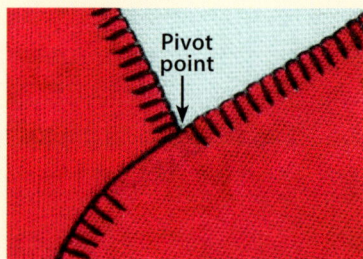

Pivot point

Photo 4

3. You can also use a machine straight stitch. Turn corners in the same manner, stitching to the corners and pivoting with needle in down position (Photo 5).

Photo 5

General Appliqué Tips

1. Use a light- to medium-weight stabilizer behind an appliqué to keep the fabric from puckering during machine stitching (Photo 6).

Photo 6

2. To reduce the stiffness of a finished appliqué, cut out the center of the fusible-web shape, leaving ¼"–½" inside the pattern line. This gives a border of adhesive to fuse to the background and leaves the center soft and easy to quilt.

3. If an appliqué fabric is so light-colored or thin that the background fabric shows through, fuse a lightweight interfacing to the wrong side of the fabric. You can also fuse a piece of the appliqué fabric to a matching piece, wrong sides together, and then apply the fusible web with a drawn pattern to one side.

Hen Party Table Topper

These appliquéd chickens are marching around the table like they expect to join the dinner party!

Skill Level
Intermediate

Finished Size
Topper Size: 27½" x 27½"

Materials
- Small piece gold tonal
- ⅛ yard white tonal
- ⅓ yard red tonal
- ⅓ yard red bandanna print
- ⅜ yard blue bandanna print
- Backing to size
- Batting to size
- 8 (³⁄₁₆"-diameter) black buttons
- Fusible web with paper release
- Lightweight fusible interfacing (optional)*
- Template material
- Thread
- Basic sewing tools and supplies

*Interfacing can be applied to make the white tonal more opaque, if needed.

Project Notes
Read all instructions before beginning this project.

Stitch right sides together using a ¼" seam allowance unless otherwise specified.

Materials and cutting lists assume 40" of usable fabric width for yardage.

Refer to the project photo and Placement Diagram for positioning of pieces and stitching lines.

Cutting

From red tonal:
- Cut 3 (2¼" by fabric width) binding strips.

From red bandanna print:
- Cut 1 (6½" by fabric width) strip.
  Subcut strip into 2 (6½") B squares.

From blue bandanna print:
- Cut 1 (10" by fabric width) strip.
  Subcut strip into 4 (10") A squares.

Completing the Topper

1. Prepare templates using the Body, Head, Wing, Leg, Tail, Comb, Beak, Flower Center, Flower Half-Center and Petal patterns provided on the insert for this project.

2. Using the prepared templates, trace the shapes onto the paper side of fusible web, referring to the list below for the number to trace. Cut shapes apart and apply to the wrong side of fabric as listed below. *Note: If background fabric shows through the white tonal, fuse lightweight interfacing to the wrong side of the white tonal before applying the shapes.*

- White tonal: 4 bodies, 4 heads, 24 petals
- Red tonal: 4 each wings, tails and combs
- Gold tonal: 4 beaks, 8 legs (4 reversed), 1 flower center, 4 flower half-centers

3. Cut out shapes on traced lines and remove paper backing.

4. Arrange hen appliqué shapes diagonally on an A square with the body in the center. The tips of the feet are positioned 1" from adjacent edges as shown in Figure 1. Tuck the top of the legs under the body with the head overlapping the body and the comb tucked under the top of the head. The tail overlaps the body at the top and the wing is placed at an angle on the body. The beak is at an angle so the hen will appear as if its head is turned sideways, facing the viewer. When satisfied with the arrangement, fuse in place.

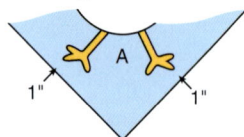

Figure 1

Here's a Tip

Even the job of "un-sewing" using a seam ripper has a few dos and don'ts that can affect your finished quilt. When you have to redo a seam, never remove stitches by pulling the edges of the fabric apart as this can stretch and distort the fabric. Instead, use your seam ripper to cut one stitch every three to four stitches. Then turn the fabric over and pull the thread on the opposite side. The thread should lift easily away from the seam. Clean up the bits of thread from the first side before restitching.

5. Machine blanket-stitch around all appliqué shapes using matching thread.

6. Arrange appliquéd A squares into two rows of two squares each with the feet positioned at the outside corners. Stitch squares into rows, and then stitch the rows together to complete the center; press.

7. Referring to Figure 2, position the flower center over the seam intersection of the A squares. Evenly arrange eight petals around the center with the petal ends tucked under the edge of the center; fuse in place.

Figure 2

8. Machine blanket-stitch around the flower appliqué using matching thread.

9. Mark a cutting line on a B square diagonally from corner to corner on the right side of fabric. Position a flower half-center almost to the line at the midway point and arrange four petals on each half, leaving a ⅜" space between the petal and the marked line as shown in Figure 3. Fuse in place. Repeat with the second B square.

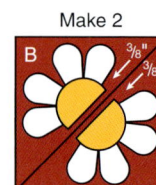

Figure 3

10. Machine blanket-stitch around the appliqués using matching thread.

11. Cut each appliquéd square in half on the drawn line to make four half-flower triangles. *Note: Completing the appliqué before cutting prevents the bias edge of the triangles from stretching while being handled during the appliqué process.*

12. Referring to Figure 4, center and stitch a half-flower triangle to one side of the center square; press seam toward triangle. Repeat, stitching a triangle to each side of the center, to complete the top.

Figure 4

13. Layer and baste the table topper referring to Quilting Basics on page 61. Quilt as desired. Model topper is stitched around each appliqué shape and echoed on each seam line.

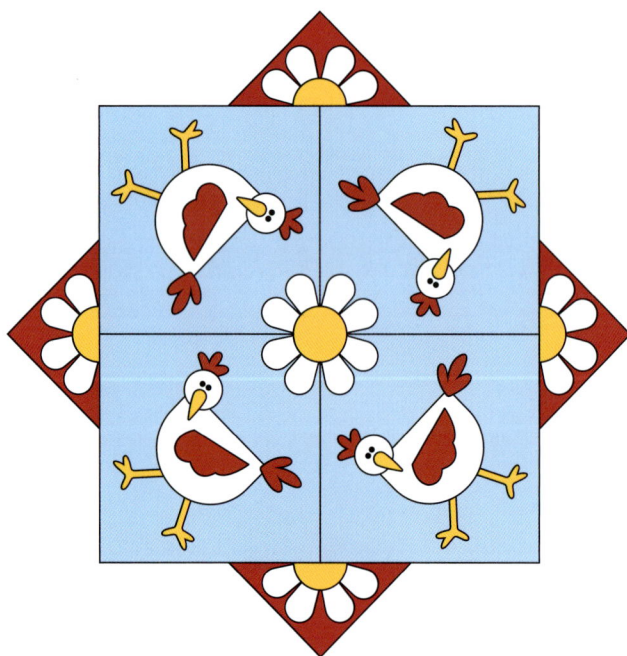

Hen Party Table Topper
Placement Diagram 27½" x 27½"

14. Prepare binding strips referring to Quilting Basics on page 61. Before applying the binding, stabilize the angle on either side of the triangles by stitching just inside the seam allowance. Clip these angles almost to the stitching as shown in Figure 5. When stitching the binding on, straighten the edge when you approach the angle with the clip instead of stopping and pivoting. When securing the binding on back of the topper, miter and fold the angle with a small tuck.

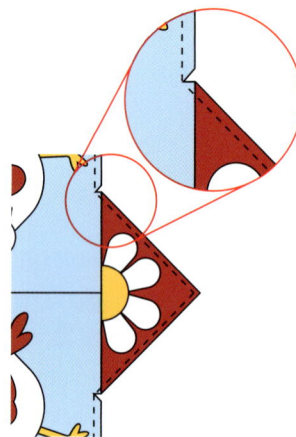

Figure 5

15. Sew two black buttons to each chicken's head for eyes. ●

Here's a Tip

This little marching chicken would look very cute on a tea towel or across the bottom of an apron. Enlarge the pattern and use it for a quilted pot holder or even a quilt block for a fun wall hanging.

Barnyard Mug Rugs

Mug rugs are like oversize coasters—plenty of room for a drink and a snack. Having this cheerful set may inspire you to take a well-deserved break!

Skill Level
Confident Beginner

Finished Size
Mug Rug Size: 8" x 6"

Materials
Materials and cutting instructions are for a set of 2 mug rugs.

- Small piece each dark pink circles, light pink mini-dot, white tonal, black-with-white dot, white-with-black dot and black solid
- Fat quarter blue tonal
- ¼ yard black-and-white stripe
- 2 (6½" x 8½") backing rectangles
- 4 (6½" x 8½") cotton batting rectangles
- 4 (³⁄₁₆"-diameter) black buttons
- Black and dark pink embroidery floss
- Embroidery needle
- Fusible web with paper release
- Template material
- Air- or water-soluble marking pen
- Thread
- Basic sewing tools and supplies

Project Notes
Read all instructions before beginning this project.

Stitch right sides together using a ¼" seam allowance unless otherwise specified.

Materials and cutting lists assume 40" of usable fabric width for yardage.

Refer to the project photo and Placement Diagram for positioning of pieces and stitching lines.

Cutting

From blue tonal:
- Cut 2 (6½" x 8½") A rectangles.

From black-and-white stripe:
- Cut 2 (2¼" by fabric width) binding strips.

Completing the Mug Rugs

1. Using pattern provided on insert, a light box or sunny window and an air- or water-soluble pen, trace the words "When Pigs Fly" on an A rectangle with the baseline of the letters centered approximately 1" up from the 8½" bottom edge (letters g and y will dip below baseline). Repeat with the words "Holy Cow!" on the remaining A rectangle.

Here's a Tip

When transferring marks for embroidery or quilting guides, always test your marker on a sample of the same fabric to be sure that the marks will come out!

2. Place each A rectangle on one batting piece and baste along the edges to secure.

3. Using two strands of black embroidery floss, backstitch on the traced lines to complete the words on each A background rectangle. Make a French knot to dot the "i" in "Pig." Sew a small cross-stitch for the bottom of the exclamation point.

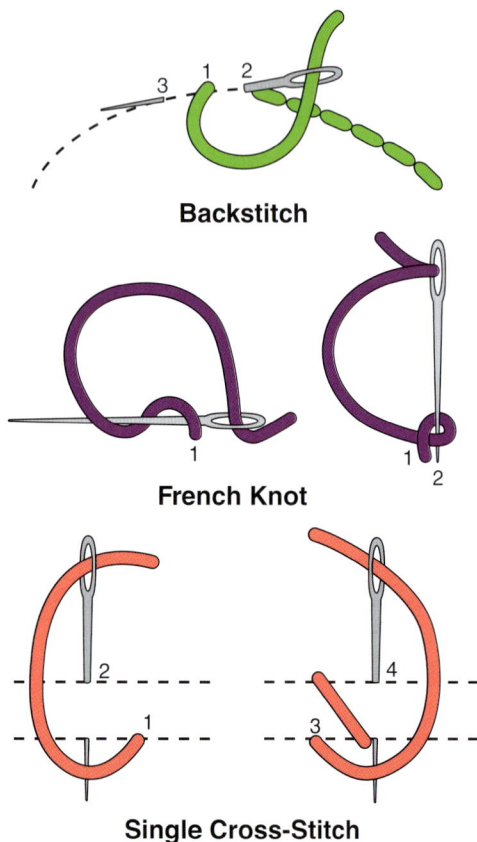

Backstitch

French Knot

Single Cross-Stitch

4. Prepare templates using the the Pig/Cow Body, Pig/Cow Leg, Pig/Cow Wing, Pig/Cow Hoof, Pig Head, Pig Snout, Cow Head, Cow Nose and Cow Udder patterns provided on the insert for this project.

5. Using the prepared templates, trace the shapes onto the paper side of fusible web, referring to information below for number to trace. Cut shapes apart and apply to wrong side of fabrics as listed below:

- Dark pink circles: 1 each pig body and pig head, 2 pig legs
- Light pink mini-dot: 1 each pig snout, cow nose and cow udder
- White tonal: 2 wings
- Black-with-white dots: 1 cow body, 2 cow legs
- White-with-black dots: 1 cow head
- Black solid: 4 hooves

6. Cut out shapes on traced lines and remove paper backing.

7. Center pig appliqué shapes above the embroidered words with the legs at an angle as shown and the hooves covering the bottoms of the legs. Tuck the wing under at the top of body and place the head with centered snout at one upper end of body. Fuse in place.

8. Center the cow appliqué shapes above the embroidered words with the legs at an angle as shown and the hooves covering the bottoms of the legs. Tuck the udder under the body just in front of the back leg and the wing at the top. Place the head at the upper end of body with the nose overlapping the bottom edge of head. Fuse in place.

9. Machine blanket-stitch around the appliqués using matching thread.

10. Transfer the pig and cow tail patterns to the back end of the bodies. Using pink floss for the pig and black for the cow, backstitch on the lines. Make three Lazy Daisy stitches at the end of the cow tail. Make two French knots for nostrils on the pig snout and the cow nose, using two strands of black floss.

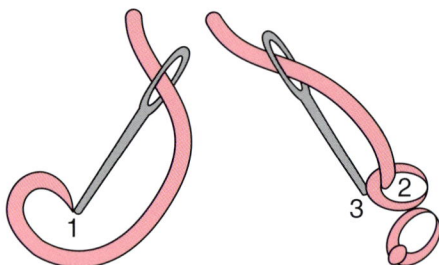

Lazy Daisy Stitch

11. Layer the backing, right side down, a batting rectangle and the appliquéd pig top, right side up. Baste to secure. Repeat for cow mug rug. Quilt by stitching around the appliqué shapes. Add other quilting as desired.

12. Prepare binding strips referring to Quilting Basics on page 61 and bind the mug rugs.

13. Sew two black buttons to each head for eyes. ●

Here's a Tip

Mug rugs are a wonderful go-to gift when you need something quickly. If you don't have time to add the appliqué motif, just make a mug rug with a fabric in the recipient's favorite colors—maybe even a novelty print of a favorite theme. Fill a matching mug with tea bags, candy, nuts or whatever treat you wish, and you'll have a thoughtful and useful gift in no time!

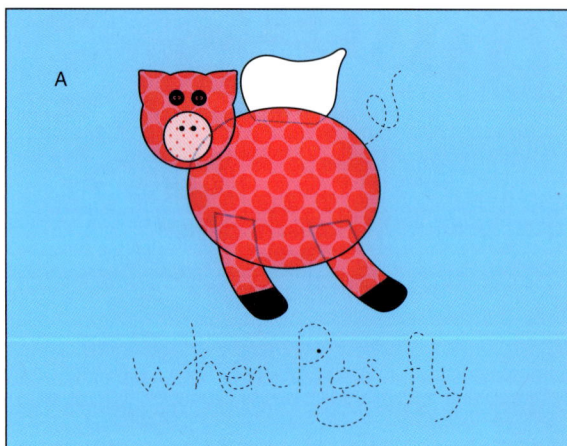

Barnyard Mug Rugs
When Pigs Fly
Placement Diagram 8" x 6"

Barnyard Mug Rugs
Holy Cow!
Placement Diagram 8" x 6"

Quilt 'Til the Cows Come Home Table Runner

Looks like the cows are home and waiting for dinner! This table runner would also make a fun wall hanging above the mantel or buffet.

Skill Level
Confident Beginner

Finished Size
Runner Size: 49½" x 16½"
Block Size: 8" x 8"
Number of Blocks: 3

Materials
- Scraps each light coral and gold tonals, and black solid
- ⅛ yard each dark coral tonal and gray dot
- ¼ yard white speckled print
- ⅓ yard total assorted green prints and tonals
- ⅜ yard green-with-white-and-blue print
- ⅞ yard total assorted blue prints and tonals
- Backing to size
- Batting to size
- 6 (⁷⁄₁₆"-diameter) black buttons
- 6 (¼"-diameter) pink buttons
- 3 (¼"-diameter) gold buttons
- Fusible web with paper release
- Template material
- Thread
- Basic sewing tools and supplies

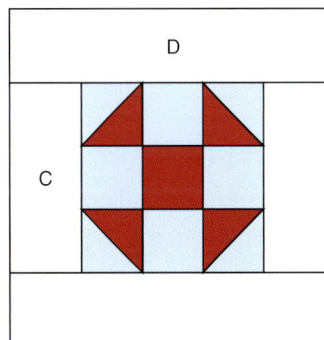

Framed Shoofly
8" x 8" Finished Block
Make 3

Project Notes
Read all instructions before beginning this project.

Stitch right sides together using a ¼" seam allowance unless otherwise specified.

Materials and cutting lists assume 40" of usable fabric width for yardage.

Refer to the project photo and Placement Diagram for positioning of pieces and stitching lines.

Cutting

From dark coral tonal:
- Cut 1 (2½" by fabric width) strip.
    Subcut strip into 6 (2½") E squares and
        3 (2") F squares.

From gray dot:
- Cut 1 (2½" by fabric width) strip.
    Subcut strip into 6 (2½") G squares and
        12 (2") H squares.

From white speckled print:
- Cut 2 (2¼" by fabric width) strips. Subcut strips into 6 each 2¼" x 5" C and 2¼" x 8" D strips.

From assorted green prints & tonals:
- Cut 66 (2") B squares.

From green-with-white-and-blue print:
- Cut 4 (2¼" by fabric width) binding strips.

From assorted blue prints & tonals:
- Cut 33 (5") A squares.

Completing the Runner

1. Arrange the A squares into three rows of 11 squares each. Sew the squares together in each row; press seams open (for a flatter surface for the fusible appliqué). Sew the rows together to make an A section; press seams open.

2. Arrange the B squares into two rows of 33 squares each. Sew the squares together in each row; press. Sew the two rows together to make a B section; press.

3. Sew the A section to the B section to complete the background; press.

4. Draw a diagonal line from corner to corner on the wrong side of each E square.

5. Pair a marked E square with a G square, right sides together, and stitch ¼" from both sides of the drawn line as shown in Figure 1. Cut on the line and press seam toward E to make two E-G units. Trim each unit to 2" square, matching the 45-degree line on ruler to the seam. Repeat to make a total of 12 E-G units.

G
¼"
E
E-G Units
Make 12

Figure 1

Here's a Tip

You can use the same technique of adding a simple quilt block to the center of an appliqué shape with many other shapes. A round-bodied snowman with a star block would be cute for winter, and a pumpkin or fall leaf shape with a Nine-Patch block of pretty autumn colors would be beautiful. Just make the block and add borders to prepare the fabric for the appliqué, centering the fusible web where you want it to be and handling the unit as if it is a plain piece of fabric.

6. Referring to Figure 2, arrange four H squares, four E-G units and an F square into three rows. Sew into rows, pressing the seams in alternate directions. Sew the rows together to make one center unit; press.

Center Unit

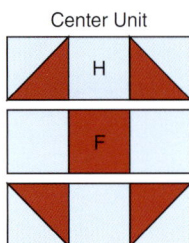

Figure 2

7. Sew C strips to opposite sides of the center unit and D strips to the top and bottom to complete one Framed Shoofly block; press seams toward C and D.

8. Repeat steps 6 and 7 to make a total of three Framed Shoofly blocks.

9. Prepare templates using the Body, Head, Ear, Nose, Leg, Hoof, Tail, Tail Tip and Cowbell patterns provided on the insert for this table runner.

Here's a Tip

When you have two sections to sew together and one section has more seams than the other, it is important that your seaming is accurate or the sections will not match. Just being slightly off, with that factor multiplied by the number of seams, can make a significant difference. There are several factors that contribute to a consistent and correct seam allowance. Cutting accurate-size pieces is the first step. Also, be sure that both raw edges are even when sewing; if the bottom piece has slipped and is not lined up with the top piece, the seam allowance will be off. The best way to improve your piecing is to measure a stitched unit and then make any adjustments needed. Sew two 3" squares together with a ¼" seam allowance. Press the seam to one side and measure your unit. It should be 5½" across. If it is not, make the necessary changes until your unit is correct.

10. Using the prepared templates, trace shapes onto the paper side of fusible web, referring to information below for number to trace. Cut shapes apart and apply to the wrong side of selected fabrics as listed below:

- White speckled print: 3 each heads and tails; 6 ears (3 reversed) and 6 legs
- Light coral tonal: 3 noses
- Black solid: 6 hooves and 3 tail tips
- Gold tonal: 3 cowbells
- Framed Shoofly block: 3 bodies, with the block centered

11. Cut out shapes on traced lines and remove paper backing.

12. Arrange one set of cow appliqués in the center of the table runner background on the A section. Place the hooves just touching the A-B seam line and covering the bottom of the legs. Tuck the end of the tail under the back edge of the cow and the nose overlapping the front of the body. Tuck the head under the top of the nose and an ear (one reversed) at each side of the head. Place the cowbell slightly in front of the cow at an angle as shown in the Placement Diagram. When all is arranged, fuse in place.

13. Position the remaining two cow motifs at opposite ends of the table runner, with the bodies about 6" from the center cow. Fuse in place.

14. Machine blanket-stitch around each appliqué using matching thread.

15. Refer to Quilting Basics on page 61 to layer and baste the table runner. Stitch around the appliqué shapes and add a double-stitched gold line from the cowbell to the cow just under the nose. Add any other quilting as desired. Project model has diagonal grid stitching in the B section and a Shoofly outline stitched in some of the A squares.

16. Prepare binding strips referring to Quilting Basics on page 61 and bind the runner.

17. Sew two black buttons to each face for eyes.

18. Sew two pink buttons to each nose for nostrils.

19. Sew a gold button just below each cowbell for a clapper. ●

**Quilt 'Til the Cows Come Home
Table Runner**
Placement Diagram 49½" x 16½"

Coming Out of My Shell Coaster Set

A set of bright, fun coasters can dress up a table or make a cute hostess gift. This set goes together quickly and can be made in any color scheme to match the decor.

Skill Level
Confident Beginner

Finished Size
Coaster Size: 4½" diameter

Materials
Materials and cutting instructions are for a set of 4 coasters.

- Small pieces light green dot, 4 floral prints and dark green dot
- Fat quarter each yellow tonal and gray crosshatch tonal
- Cotton batting scraps
- 4 (¼"-diameter) light green buttons
- 8 (½"–⅝"-diameter) blue, pink and yellow flower-shaped buttons
- Fusible web with paper release
- Template material
- Thread
- Basic sewing tools and supplies

Project Notes
Read all instructions before beginning this project.

Stitch right sides together using a ¼" seam allowance unless otherwise specified.

Materials and cutting lists assume 40" of usable fabric width for yardage.

Refer to the project photo and Placement Diagram for positioning of pieces and stitching lines.

Cutting

From light green dot:
- Cut 4 (1½" x 5½") B strips.

From yellow tonal:
- Cut 2¼"-wide bias binding strips to equal 90" when joined.

From gray crosshatch tonal:
- Cut 3 (5½" x 20") strips.
    Subcut strips into 4 (4½" x 5½") A rectangles and 4 (5½") backing squares.

From cotton batting scraps:
- Cut 8 (5½") squares.

Here's a Tip

Cutting binding on the bias grain is useful for finishing curved edges. Because there is more stretch in a bias binding, it will ease comfortably around the curves. And because of this elasticity, handle it carefully so it does not over-stretch and ripple.

Completing the Coasters

1. Join an A and B piece along 5½" edges as shown in Figure 1 to make an A-B unit; press seam toward B. Repeat to make a total of 4 A-B units.

A-B Unit
Make 4

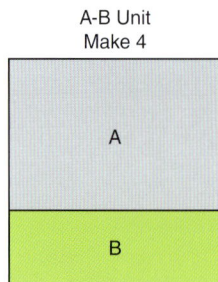

A

B

Figure 1

2. Place each A-B unit on one batting square and baste around the edges to secure.

3. Prepare templates using the Shell, Head, Tail and Coaster Circle patterns provided on the insert for this project.

4. Using the prepared templates for the shell, head and tail, trace the shapes onto the paper side of fusible web, referring to information below for number to trace. Cut shapes apart and apply to the wrong side of fabrics as listed below:

• 4 floral prints: 1 shell from each print
• Dark green dot: 4 each heads and tails

Here's a Tip

• *Did you know you can make darling note cards with your fabric and fusible web? You could use this turtle motif (it's perfect for a belated birthday wish), preparing the appliqué just as you would for the coasters. Fuse the motif to the front of a purchased plain note card, and if you wish, you can even finish it with machine straight stitches sewn close to the edge. Use an old machine needle as sewing through paper dulls a new one quickly. Add a few more design lines with the machine stitching, such as a line for the ground and maybe a cloud in the sky, and you'll have a fun and unique card to send!*

5. Cut out shapes on traced lines and remove paper backing.

6. Place one shell on each A-B unit with the bottom edge on the seam line. Tuck the head and tail under the edge of the shell on opposite sides. Fuse in place.

7. Machine blanket-stitch around the appliqués using matching thread.

8. Layer a backing square, right side down, a batting square and the appliquéd top, right side up. Pin or baste to secure. Quilt by stitching around the appliqué shapes. Repeat for all four coasters.

9. Referring to Figure 2, center and mark a 5"-diameter circle on the front of each coaster, using the prepared coaster circle template; machine-baste ⅛" in from the drawn line. Cut out on the drawn line.

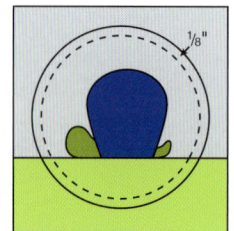

Figure 2

10. Prepare bias binding referring to Quilting Basics on page 61. Apply binding to edges.

11. Sew a green button to each head for an eye.

12. Sew two flower-shaped buttons to the green section under each turtle. ●

Coming Out of My Shell Coaster Set
Placement Diagram 4½" diameter

Songbird Pillow

This pillow features a cheery pieced bird walking through a field of flowers. The music fabric suggests he has a lot to sing about!

Skill Level

Beginner

Finished Size

Pillow Size: 12" x 12"
Block Size: 12" x 12"
Number of Blocks: 1

Materials

- Scraps yellow, blue and orange tonals
- Small piece cream music score
- ⅓ yard red tonal
- ½ yard gray tonal
- 12½" x 12½" batting square plus scrap for wing
- Green No. 5 pearl cotton or embroidery floss
- 1 (⁵⁄₁₆"-diameter) dark gray button
- 12" x 12" pillow form
- Small (30mm) yo-yo maker (optional)
- Thread
- Basic sewing tools and supplies

Songbird
12" x 12" Finished Block
Make 1

Project Notes

Read all instructions before beginning this project.

Stitch right sides together using a ¼" seam allowance unless otherwise specified.

Materials and cutting lists assume 40" of usable fabric width for yardage.

Refer to the project photo and Placement Diagram for positioning of pieces and stitching lines.

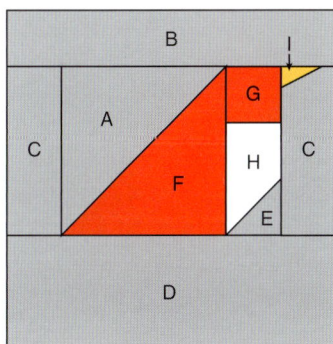

Cutting

If not using a yo-yo maker, use Yo-Yo Flower pattern provided in the insert to prepare a template to cut circles for yo-yo flowers.

From yellow tonal:

- Cut 1 (2" x 2½") I rectangle.
- Cut 2 (3⅛") squares for yo-yo maker or 2 (2½") circles using prepared template.

From blue & orange tonals:

- From each color, cut 2 (3⅛") squares for yo-yo maker or 2 (2½") circles using prepared template.

Here's a Tip

Make enough of these pieced bird blocks for a quilt, perhaps making each bird with a different fabric. Or make several pillows to set on a bench or love seat for the porch or entry.

From cream music score:
- Cut 1 (2½" x 4½") H rectangle.

From red tonal:
- Cut 1 (6⅞" by fabric width) strip.
  Subcut strip into 1 (6⅞") F square, 2 (3½" x 5½") wing rectangles, 1 (2½") G square and 2 (3⅛") squares for yo-yo maker or 2 (2½") circles using prepared template.

From gray tonal:
- Cut 1 (12½" by fabric width) strip.
  Subcut strip into 2 (9" x 12½") J rectangles, 1 each 4½" x 12½" D and 2½" x 12½" B strip, 1 (6⅞") A square, 2 (2½" x 6½") C strips and 1 (2½") E square.

Completing the Pillow

1. Draw a diagonal line from corner to corner on the wrong side of the F and E squares.

2. Pair the A and F squares, right sides together, and sew ¼" on each side of the drawn line as shown in Figure 1. Cut apart on the drawn line to make two A-F units; discard one unit. Press seam toward F.

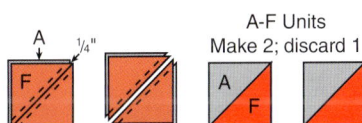

Figure 1

3. Referring to Figure 2, position an E square on one end of H, right sides together, and stitch just slightly below the drawn line. Trim the seam to ¼"; open and press the seam toward E to make an E-H unit.

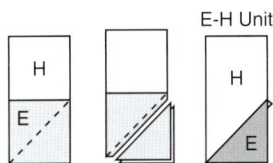

Figure 2   **Figure 3**

4. Measure 1" down on one short side and 1¾" across the adjacent long side of the I rectangle on the wrong side and mark each location with a dot. Connect the two dots to make a stitching line as shown in Figure 3.

5. Referring to Figure 4, position I on a C strip, right sides together, and stitch on the drawn line. Trim the seam to ¼", flip open and press toward I to make a C-I unit. Trim edges of I to match the corner of C.

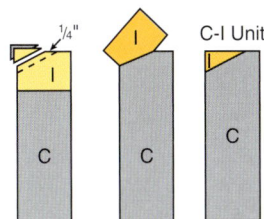

Figure 4

6. Arrange and stitch a G square to the H end of the E-H unit to make a G-E-H unit; press.

7. Arrange the remaining C strip, A-F unit, G-E-H unit and C-I unit as shown in Figure 5. Sew together to make the bird body; press.

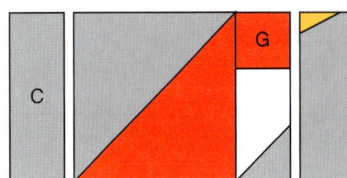

Figure 5

8. Referring to the block drawing, sew the B strip to the top and the D strip to the bottom to complete the Songbird block.

9. Prepare a template using the Wing pattern provided on the insert for this project and trace the shape on the wrong side of a wing rectangle. Referring to Padded Appliqué on page 27, make one wing by layering the traced rectangle and remaining wing rectangle right sides together on a batting scrap. Stitch all around, cutting a slash for turning. Trim seams, turn, press edges flat and whipstitch opening closed. Topstitch all around ¼" from the edge to complete the wing.

10. Place the pillow top right side up on the batting square and baste around the edges to secure.

11. Quilt by stitching in the ditch around the bird. Transfer the legs pattern and double-stitch with black thread.

12. Referring to Figure 6, position the wing, slash side down, on the back of the bird at an angle.

Making Yo-Yos

To make any size yo-yo:

1. Trace size circle desired or indicated on pattern using a template on wrong side of fabric.

2. Cut a length of thread in a color to match fabric; double thread and knot ends together.

3. Working with wrong side of yo-yo circle facing you, turn fabric under ¼" to wrong side and insert needle near the folded edge as shown in Figure A.

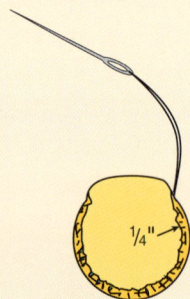

¼"

Figure A

4. Stitch a running stitch, using approximately ⅜"-long stitches, around the edge of the circle, turning fabric edge under as you sew referring to Figure B. Stop stitching when you reach the beginning knot.

Figure B

5. Pull thread to gather the circle as tightly as you can (or as desired) and move the hole to the center of the circle as seen in Figure C.

Figure C

6. Insert needle between two gathers to the back of the yo-yo and make several small knots to secure; clip thread.

Attach wing by sewing on top of the topstitching line on the curved end, leaving the tip free.

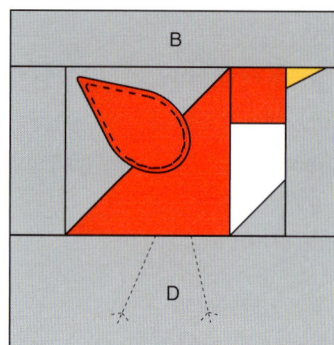

Figure 6

13. Sew the button to the head for an eye.

14. Using one strand of green pearl cotton or six strands of embroidery floss, sew a running stitch across the pillow just below the bird's feet (approximately 1¾" up from the bottom edge).

15. If using a yo-yo maker, follow the manufacturer's directions or refer to Making Yo-Yos on this page to make eight yo-yo flowers with red, blue, yellow and orange fabrics.

Here's a Tip

There are several ways to attach yo-yo flowers to a background, and they each give a distinctive look to the project. First, it can be helpful to secure the placement by using a small dab of fabric glue to prevent the yo-yo from shifting. The edges can then be sewn down with an invisible appliqué stitch, as shown on this pillow, or you can attach with a bold running stitch around the edges using a contrasting color of thread or with a blanket stitch or feather stitch. You can also attach a yo-yo by sewing a button to the center hole, sewing down through the background and leaving the edges loose.

16. Arrange the yo-yo flowers across the bottom of the pillow as shown. Use a small appliqué stitch to hand-sew the edges down.

17. To make an envelope back for the pillow, press and stitch a ¼" double hem on one long side of each J rectangle. Place pillow front right side up and position one J rectangle at the top, right side down, matching top raw edges. Place second J rectangle at the bottom edge, right side down, matching raw edges at the bottom and overlapping the first J rectangle. Stitch all around with a ¼" seam allowance. Turn right side out through the overlapped opening.

18. Insert the pillow form into the pillowcase to finish. ●

Songbird Pillow
Placement Diagram 12" x 12"

Padded Appliqué

Some of the projects are finished with a "padded" appliqué. In this technique, an appliqué piece is sewn with two layers of fabric and a layer of batting and then turned right side out through an opening. Padded appliqué gives dimensional interest to a project. Refer to Quilting Basics on page 61 for details about preparing templates from patterns.

1. Prepare template using pattern provided and trace the shape on the wrong side of the selected fabric. Fold the fabric in half with the right sides facing and the traced shape on top.

2. Pin this fabric to a scrap of batting that is slightly larger than traced shape and then sew on the traced lines as shown in Figure A.

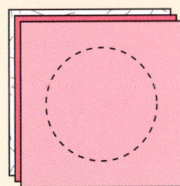

Figure A

3. The instructions will tell you whether you should leave a side opening for turning in the seam allowance, or if you should sew all around and then make a slash in one layer of fabric only for turning.

4. Cut out the shape ⅛"–¼" from the seam line, clip curves generously (or use pinking shears to cut out).

5. To make a slash, pinch the top layer of fabric and pull away that layer from the other fabric layer; make a little snip in the pinched fabric. Insert scissor tips into the hole and cut the fabric just enough to turn the shape right side out (Figure B). If desired, add a little no-fray solution to the cut edges of the slash and let it dry.

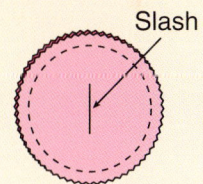

Slash

Figure B

6. After turning the shape right side out through the slash or side opening, whipstitch the cut edges of slash back together as shown in Figure C or slip-stitch the side opening closed. Press the shape from the top side so it is flat and smooth at the edges.

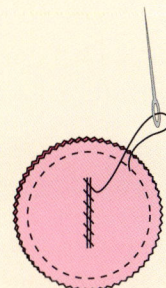

Figure C

Horse of a Different Color

Playing with color is always fun! Add some cute horses and wonky stars, and you'll have a quilt to brighten the room and the mood.

Quilted by Jean McDaniel

Skill Level
Confident Beginner

Finished Size
Quilt Size: 48" x 48"
Block Size: 10" x 10"
Number of Blocks: 9

Materials
- Small piece black tonal
- ⅛ yard each 16 assorted-color tonals
- ¼ yard each 9 assorted-color tonals
- 1⅝ yards dark gray tonal
- 1⅞ yards white-with-gray print
- Backing to size
- Batting to size
- 9 (⁵⁄₁₆"-diameter) black buttons
- Fusible web with paper release
- Template material
- Thread
- Basic sewing tools and supplies

Project Notes
Read all instructions before beginning this project.

Stitch right sides together using a ¼" seam allowance unless otherwise specified.

Materials and cutting lists assume 40" of usable fabric width for yardage.

Refer to the project photo and Placement Diagram for positioning of pieces and stitching lines.

Horse
10" x 10" Finished Block
Make 9

Cutting

From each of 16 assorted-color tonals:
- Cut 1 (3½") C square.
- Cut 4 (3½") squares.
   Cut each square in half on 1 diagonal to make 8 F triangles.

From dark gray tonal:
- Cut 8 (3½" by fabric width) strips.
   Subcut strips into 24 (3½" x 10½") B strips.
- Cut 6 (2¼" by fabric width) binding strips.

From white-with-gray print:
- Cut 3 (10½" by fabric width) strips.
   Subcut strips into 9 (10½") A squares.
- Cut 6 (3½" by fabric width) strips.
   Subcut strips into 12 (3½" x 10½") D strips and 20 (3½") E squares.

Completing the Blocks

1. Choose one color tonal from the nine assorted-color tonals for each of the nine body and back legs shapes and a contrasting color for the tail, mane and forelock.

2. Prepare templates using the Body, Front and Rear Back Legs, Tail, Mane, Forelock and Hoof patterns provided on the insert for this quilt.

3. Using the prepared templates, trace the shapes onto the paper side of fusible web, referring to information below for number to trace. Cut shapes apart and apply to the wrong side of selected fabrics as listed below:

- 9 assorted-color tonals: 9 bodies; 1 each rear and front back leg to match each body.
- 9 contrasting colored tonals: 1 each tail, mane and forelock
- Black tonal: 36 hooves

4. Cut out shapes on traced lines and remove paper backing.

5. Referring to the block drawing, position body 1½" from bottom edge of an A square; tuck a tail, mane, and rear and front back legs under the edge of the horse and place the forelock on top of the head. Fuse in place. Cover the bottom end of each leg with a hoof; fuse in place. Repeat to make a total of nine blocks.

6. Machine blanket-stitch around each appliqué shape using matching thread.

Here's a Tip

When doing the stitch-and-flip method for the star points, it is very important to check that the triangle completely covers the corner before trimming the seam. Press the seam very flat before trimming so the resulting square or rectangle is accurate.

Completing the Quilt

1. Before assembly, lay out the entire quilt for positioning of the sashing and star points. Arrange the nine horse blocks into three rows of three blocks each and position B strips, C squares, D strips and E squares as shown in Figure 1.

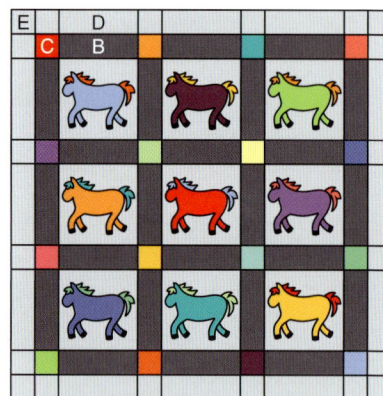

Figure 1

2. Distribute matching F triangles at each intersection to coordinate with the C squares. Select one B strip or E square and two F triangles. Referring to Figure 2, position an F triangle across one corner of the strip or square, right sides together, and stitch ¼" from the edge of F. Fold the triangle over, making sure it completely covers the corner; press. Trim the excess F even with the edges of the B strip or E square.

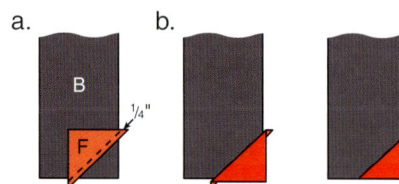

Figure 2

3. Repeat the stitching process in step 2 to add a matching F triangle to the adjacent corner of the B or E piece to complete one set of star points as shown in Figure 3. Place the B or E piece back into the quilt layout.

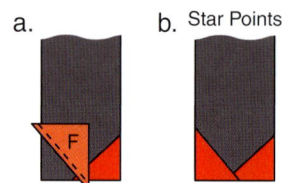

Figure 3

4. Repeat steps 2 and 3 to add two points to each edge of the B or E pieces that touch a C square.

5. Sew the strips, squares and blocks together in each row; press.

6. Sew the rows together to complete the quilt top; press.

7. Refer to Quilting Basics on page 61 to layer and baste the quilt. Stitch around the appliqué shapes and stitch the contour lines on the bodies, referring to the pattern. Complete quilting as desired.

Here's a Tip

File this "wonky star" sashing design in your repertoire of finishes because it's fun to do and it definitely adds pizzazz to a quilt. To make a truly quick-and-easy quilt, cut plain squares out of assorted colors, add sashing strips of contrasting color with a third color for the star points.

8. Prepare binding strips referring to Quilting Basics on page 61 and bind the quilt.

9. Sew a black button to each horse for eyes. ●

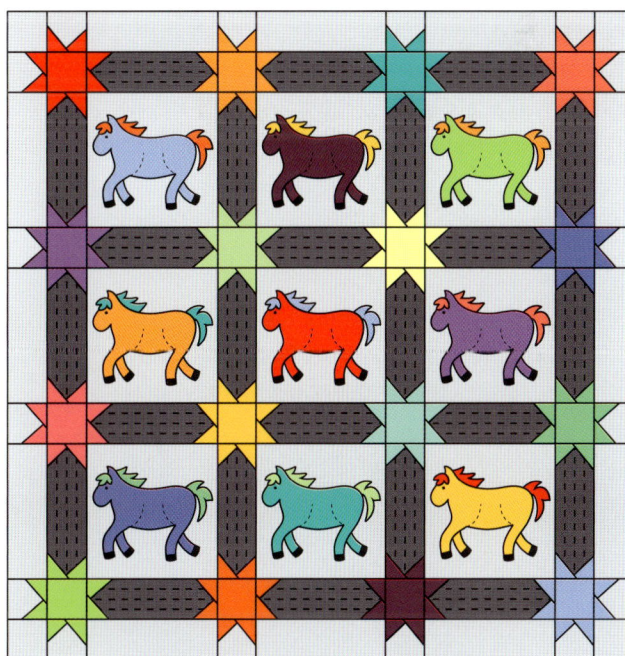

Horse of a Different Color
Placement Diagram 48" x 48"

A Good Book Is Food for Thought

You can whip this bookmark up in a jiffy. Why not make one for yourself and a few for gifts?

Skill Level
Beginner

Finished Size
Bookmark Size: 3" x 7½"

Materials
- Scraps green tonal and cream solid
- Small pieces gray tonal and orange-with-brown dots
- 3" x 7½" batting
- 3" x 7½" fusible interfacing
- 2 (¼"-diameter) brown buttons
- Fusible web with paper release
- Template material
- Thread
- Basic sewing tools and supplies

Here's a Tip
When I think of giraffes, I think "tall," so a giraffe would be a perfect motif for a quilted growth chart. Enlarge the patterns and cut the neck as wide and as tall as you need for your wall hanging!

Project Notes
Read all instructions before beginning this project.

Stitch right sides together using a ¼" seam allowance unless otherwise specified.

Refer to the project photo and Placement Diagram for positioning of pieces and stitching lines.

Cutting

From gray tonal:
- Cut 2 (3" x 7½") A rectangles.

Completing the Bookmark
1. Baste batting to wrong side of one A rectangle and fuse interfacing to the wrong side of the remaining A rectangle for the back.

2. Prepare templates using the Neck, Head, Ear, Horn and Leaf patterns provided on the insert for this project.

3. Using the prepared templates, trace shapes onto the paper side of fusible web, referring to information below for number to trace. Cut shapes apart and apply to the wrong side of fabric as listed below:

- Orange-with-brown dots: 1 each neck and head, 2 ears (1 reversed)
- Cream solid: 2 horns
- Green tonal: 3 leaves

th her on the couch. "Therese is the one who
n."

would be the one listed as the p...
s she transferred it, in whic...
a claim on it. If t...
anything. It coul...
he presented it as...
d me that inform...
fidential," Annie sa...
other sip of coc...

y what happened to t...
to have." Annie ran h...
assuming that the dau...
could be someone ent...
is a leap because they...
le did say the daughter...
ppened to the husband.

right about that," Annie s...
w is why they were in Stor...
hat is the key." Annie leane...
of the couch. "So where does...

ugged and took a final swig of...
hat collection of old *Points*. W...
w and look through his newspa-
rese Marie Gilkerson who died...
encyclopedia about the local
nething."

Annie rose to her feet and wandered toward a
dow. She crossed her arms over her body. "I do
thing. I will welcome the day I can return those sto
tes to Joan or Therese or whoever has a claim c
he distance, the huge silhouette of a dark Gre
red. "And I can have my house back."
utching her empty cup, Alice came and stoo
"It's still a beautiful house. Betsy made it a p
nd welcome, and you have done the same t
shook her head. "I don't know about that.
like that silly mouse to big things like so
it just doesn't feel like it."
ped an arm around Annie's back and gav
eeze.
elled up in Annie. "Thanks for putting
" She cast her gaze downward. No ma
nds who were true treasures.
he mug in her hand fell to the floor.
ked up and followed the line of Alice
hand fluttered to her neck. A sing
of Grey Gables bounced across thei
der must have gone up to the attic
fficer searched the second floor. "If
free rein to the whole house."
ck certificates there." Alice bolt-
d to call the police."
's sleeve. "OK, but we need to
police get here, the intruder

4. Cut out shapes on traced lines and remove paper backing.

5. Position the giraffe neck at the center bottom of the right side of the A/batting front piece; fuse in place. Arrange the head at the top of the neck with the horns at the top at an angle and an ear on each side as shown. Fuse in place.

6. Machine blanket-stitch around the appliqué shapes using matching thread.

7. Position the leaves with two above the head and one at the side, just below the head. Fuse in place and machine blanket-stitch around the edges with green thread. With the same green thread, stitch stems, one to connect the two top leaves as if the branch is bending down from the top right edge and the other just under the head as if the giraffe is eating it.

8. Sew the buttons to the head for eyes.

9. Layer the A/interfacing bookmark back, right side down, and the front, right side up, and carefully line up the edges. Hand-baste about ¼" from the edge. Machine-stitch a close zigzag stitch all around with matching thread. Stitch around two or three times for a nice full finish. ●

A Good Book Is Food for Thought
Placement Diagram 3" x 7½"

Here's a Tip

Fabric postcards are a fun and popular craft, and they can be made in much the same way as this bookmark. If you wish to make it stiffer, simply use a firmer interfacing.

Flamingo Scissors Case

This colorful and well-padded scissors holder is big enough for a full-size pair of scissors and a rotary cutter. Two buttons serve for the body and head, so the appliqué goes together very quickly!

Skill Level
Beginner

Finished Size
Case Size: 4½" x 9½", including binding

Materials
- Scraps dark pink and orange solids
- Small pieces pink floral and yellow tonal
- ⅓ yard light pink solid
- Small piece batting
- 2 (¼"-diameter) pink buttons
- 1 (⅞"-diameter) pink button
- 1 (1½"-diameter) pink button
- Fusible web with paper release
- Template material
- Thread
- Basic sewing tools and supplies

Project Notes
Read all instructions before beginning this project.

Stitch right sides together using a ¼" seam allowance unless otherwise specified.

Materials and cutting lists assume 40" of usable fabric width for yardage.

Refer to the project photo and Placement Diagram for positioning of pieces and stitching lines.

Cutting

From pink floral:
- Cut 2 (4½" x 9½") A rectangles.

From yellow tonal:
- Cut 1 (4½" x 6¼") B rectangle.

From light pink solid:
- Cut 1 (2½" by fabric width) binding strip.
- Cut 1 (4½" by fabric width) strip.
  Subcut strip into 1 (4½" x 7") C rectangle.

From batting:
- Cut 1 each 4½" x 9½" and 4½" x 6¼" rectangle.

Completing the Case

1. Baste the same-size batting rectangles to the wrong side of one A and the B rectangle.

2. Prepare templates using the Neck, Tail and Beak patterns provided on the insert for this project.

3. Using the prepared templates, trace the shape onto the paper side of fusible web, referring to information below for number to trace. Cut shapes apart and apply to the wrong side of fabrics as listed below:

- Dark pink solid: 1 each neck and tail
- Orange solid: 1 beak

4. Cut out shapes on traced lines and remove paper backing.

5. Referring to Figure 1, position the two large pink buttons on the B pocket front with the largest body button about 2½" up from the bottom edge and 1⅜" from the right edge. Place the head button about ⅝" down from the top edge and 1⅛" from the left edge.

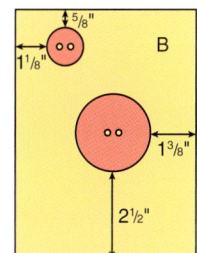

Figure 1

6. Slip the ends of the neck appliqué under the buttons and the tail under the body button on the right. Slip the end of the beak under the edge of the head button. Adjust the buttons and pieces as necessary so the ends of the appliqués are fully covered. When satisfied with the arrangement, remove the buttons, fuse the appliqués in place and then machine blanket-stitch the edges of the appliqués using matching thread.

7. Sew the C rectangle to the top of the appliquéd pocket front, right sides facing and matching the top raw edges as shown in Figure 2. Flip the C rectangle over to the wrong side of the pocket and match the sides and bottom edges, forming a narrow border at the top front. Press and baste the edges together.

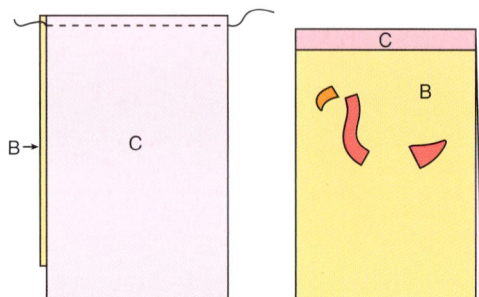

Figure 2

8. Finish the pocket by stitching around the appliqués and stitching in the ditch of the B-C seam. Transfer the quilting pattern for legs and double-stitch the legs with pink thread.

Here's a Tip

When quilting lines are part of the design and you want to make them stand out, use a thread color that will contrast with the background and stitch twice on the design lines.

9. Sew the body and head buttons in place and sew the two small pink buttons to the legs for the joints.

10. Layer the two A rectangles with right sides out and the batting in between. Pin or baste to hold. Quilt a grid or as desired to finish the back of the holder.

11. Pin the pocket to the back, matching the bottom and side edges; machine-baste to secure.

12. Prepare the binding strip referring to Quilting Basics on page 61 and bind the edges to complete the holder. ●

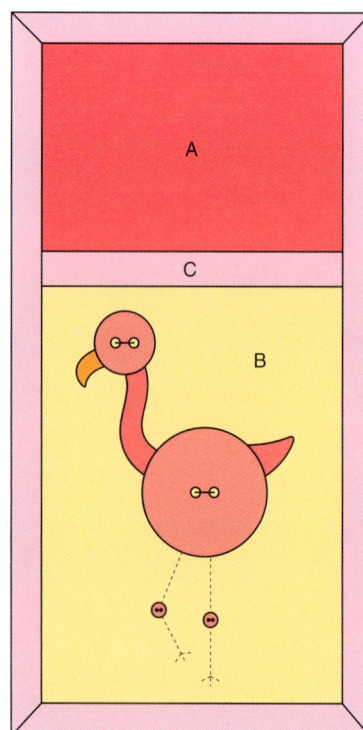

Flamingo Scissors Case
Placement Diagram 4½" x 9½",
including binding

Here's a Tip

You can use the same construction steps to make silverware holders for the table or buffet. If you do not want an appliqué on the front, just choose two or three coordinating fabrics that will enhance your table setting.

Counting Sheep

These frisky sheep are leaping over the fence, not to put you to sleep but to brighten your day! Simple appliqué with fun fabrics and a few yo-yo flowers make this a quick and easy wall hanging.

Skill Level
Beginner

Finished Size
Wall Hanging Size: 8" x 38½"
Block Size: 8" x 6"
Number of Blocks: 6

Materials
- Small piece each white tonal and black solid
- Small piece each 5 bright florals: orange, blue, purple, yellow and red
- ⅛ yard green-with-blue dots
- ⅛ yard green floral
- ⅝ yard light blue tonal
- Backing to size
- Batting to size
- 10 (⁵⁄₁₆"-diameter) white buttons
- Small (30mm) yo-yo maker (optional)
- Fusible web with paper release
- Template material
- Thread
- Basic sewing tools and supplies

Project Notes
Read all instructions before beginning this project.

Stitch right sides together using a ¼" seam allowance unless otherwise specified.

Materials and cutting lists assume 40" of usable fabric width for yardage.

Refer to the project photo and Placement Diagram for positioning of pieces and stitching lines.

Sheep
8" x 6" Finished Block
Make 5

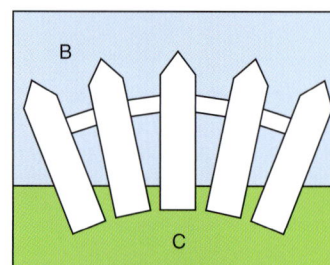

Fence
8" x 6" Finished Block
Make 1

Cutting

From 5 bright florals:
- Cut 7 (3⅛") squares for yo-yo maker or 7 (2½") circles using provided pattern on insert.

From green-with-blue dots:
- Cut 2 (1" by fabric width) strips.
  Subcut strips into 5 (1" x 8½") D strips.

From green floral:
- Cut 1 (2½" x 8½") C rectangle.

From light blue tonal:
- Cut 3 (2¼" by fabric width) binding strips.
- Cut 1 (8½" by fabric width) strip.
  Subcut strip into 5 (6½" x 8½") A and
  1 (4½" x 8½") B rectangles.

Completing the Blocks

1. Prepare templates using the Body, Tail, Head, Front and Back Legs, and Fence Post and Rail patterns provided on the insert for this wall hanging.

2. Using prepared templates, trace the shapes onto the paper side of fusible web, referring to information below for number to trace. Cut shapes apart and apply to the wrong side of fabrics as listed below:

- Bright florals: 5 bodies (2 reversed)
- Black solid: 5 heads; 5 tails (2 reversed) and 5 each front and back legs (2 sets reversed)
- White tonal: 5 fence posts and 4 rails

Here's a Tip

An appliqué pressing sheet is not essential for fusing but it certainly makes the process easier. It allows you to arrange the entire set of shapes for one block, tack them together with heat, and then remove them to fuse the motif to the background fabric. To use the pressing sheet, place the pattern under the sheet. Remove the paper backing from the cut-out shapes and arrange them over the pressing sheet, using the pattern as a guide. Then, simply press the shapes so they adhere wherever they overlap. Let the appliqués cool before removing them from the sheet and repositioning them on the background fabric.

3. Cut out shapes on traced lines and remove paper backing.

4. Position a sheep body on an A rectangle with the bottom of the sheep 1¼" from the bottom 8½" edge of the rectangle. Arrange the front and back legs at an angle as shown with the tops tucked under the edge of the body. Place the head at an angle, overlapping the body and the tail tucked under the edge of the body at the other end. Fuse in place. Repeat with the remaining sheep appliqués and

A rectangles to make a total of five sheep motifs. *Note: Two sheep are facing the opposite direction (the two reversed motifs) and the head angle varies slightly on each sheep.*

5. Sew the B and C rectangles together along the 8½" edges to make a B-C unit; press the seam open.

6. Arrange the fence posts and rails on the B-C unit with the posts slanting toward the sides as shown in the block drawing. Place a rail between the posts with the edges under the posts. Fuse in place.

7. Machine blanket-stitch the edges of all the appliqué shapes, using matching thread, to complete one Fence block and five Sheep blocks.

Completing the Wall Hanging

1. Arrange the five Sheep blocks in a vertical row with the Fence block at the bottom; place D strips between the blocks. Sew together to complete the wall hanging top; press.

2. Refer to Quilting Basics on page 61 to layer and baste the quilt. Stitch around the appliqué shapes and add other quilting as desired.

3. Prepare binding strips referring to Quilting Basics on page 61 and bind the wall quilt.

4. If using a yo-yo maker, follow the manufacturer's directions or refer to Making Yo-Yos on page 26 to make seven yo-yo flowers.

Here's a Tip

You can change the look of this appliquéd wall hanging, or any appliqués, by using different fabric styles. You can also change the look by making changes in the blanket stitching on the edges. Use a contrasting-color thread so the stitching becomes more decorative. Or substitute a 40-wt. black thread to give a folk-art look to the appliqué. You can also blanket-stitch by hand with embroidery floss or pearl cotton.

5. Arrange the yo-yo flowers across the bottom of the Fence block. Hand-sew the edges down to secure.

6. Sew two white buttons to each sheep face for eyes to finish. ●

Counting Sheep
Placement Diagram 8" x 38½"

Dream Big, Little One

Sleepy whales swim across this baby quilt, full of dreams for a big day!

Skill Level
Beginner

Finished Size
Quilt Size: 36" x 54"

Materials
- Small pieces aqua, gray and coral tonals
- 1⅓ yards total assorted ocean-themed aqua, gray, coral and tan prints and tonals
- 1⅜ yards aqua print
- Backing to size
- Batting to size
- Fusible web with paper release
- Template material
- Thread
- Basic sewing tools and supplies

Project Notes
Read all instructions before beginning this project.

Stitch right sides together using a ¼" seam allowance unless otherwise specified.

Materials and cutting lists assume 40" of usable fabric width for yardage.

Refer to the project photo and Placement Diagram for positioning of pieces and stitching lines.

Cutting

From assorted ocean-themed prints & tonals:
- Cut 120 (3½") A squares.

From aqua print:
- Cut 4 (6½" by fabric width) strips.
  Subcut strips into 4 (6½" x 36½") B strips.
- Cut 5 (2¼" by fabric width) binding strips.

Completing the Appliqués

1. Prepare a template using the Whale pattern provided on the insert for this quilt.

2. Using prepared template, trace whale shape onto the paper side of fusible web, referring to information below for number to trace. Cut shapes apart and apply to the wrong side of fabric as listed below:

- Aqua tonal: 2 whales (1 reversed)
- Gray tonal: 2 whales (1 reversed)
- Coral tonal: 2 whales (1 reversed)

3. Cut out whale shapes on traced lines and remove paper backing.

4. Arrange the whales on the B strips as follows:

- Place one each coral and gray whale on two of the strips, using reversed shapes for the second set.
- Place an aqua whale on each of the remaining two strips, using reversed shape for the second.

Each whale is positioned ¾" up from the bottom of the strip, but the placement on the strip varies. When satisfied with the arrangement, fuse in place.

5. Transfer the smile line onto the whale appliqués. Machine blanket-stitch around each whale, continuing the stitch up the smile line as shown in Figure 1.

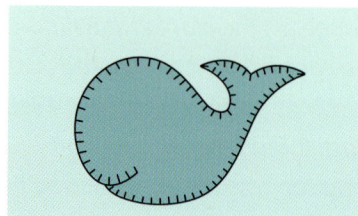

Figure 1

Completing the Quilt

1. Arrange and sew the A squares into 10 rows of 12 squares each; press.

Here's a Tip

This whale appliqué could be used in a variety of ways to make a fun, coordinated nursery. You could place whales swimming along the bottom of a curtain and add them to burp cloths, bibs, diaper bags, and even baby clothing. Reduce or enlarge the size as desired using a photocopier.

Dream Big, Little One
Placement Diagram 36" x 54"

2. Referring to Figure 2, sew two rows together to make one patchwork strip set; press. Repeat with the remaining rows to make a total of five strip sets.

Patchwork Strip Set
Make 5

Figure 2

3. Arrange the patchwork strip sets and appliquéd strips in horizontal rows, as shown in the Placement Diagram, beginning and ending with a patchwork strip set.

4. Sew the rows together to complete the top.

5. Refer to Quilting Basics on page 61 to layer and baste the quilt. Stitch around the appliqués and along the whales' smiles. Transfer the eye pattern to each whale and double-stitch on the line to make it stand out. Complete quilting as desired.

6. Prepare binding strips referring to Quilting Basics on page 61 and bind the quilt. ●

Here's a Tip

Finishing a quilt with a label that gives the quilt name, year of completion and name of quilter (and longarm quilter, if applicable) is so appreciated, especially when you are gifting the quilt. It gives your quilt its little spot in history and makes it special for anyone that may own it. An easy way to make a label is to cut a 6"–7" square and fold it in half diagonally. Write any information on one triangular half with a permanent fabric pen. After quilting, but before you add binding, place it on a bottom corner on the back, matching the raw edges to the raw edges of the quilt. Baste in place and then sew the binding down on top of the label. Hand-sew the folded edge down when you finish the binding.

Chicken Pincushion

This chicken pincushion is assembled as a Log Cabin block with felt embellishments added in the seams.

Skill Level
Beginner

Finished Size
Pincushion Size: 5" x 5"
Block Size: 5" x 5"
Number of Blocks: 1

Materials
- Scraps light and dark tan prints and tonals
- 5½" backing square
- 5½" batting square
- Wool or acrylic felt scraps red and gold
- 1 (⅛"-diameter) black button
- Red and gold embroidery floss
- Cotton or polyester fiberfill
- Template material
- Thread
- Basic sewing tools and supplies

Project Notes
Read all instructions before beginning this project.

Stitch right sides together using a ¼" seam allowance unless otherwise specified.

Refer to the project photo and Placement Diagram for positioning of pieces and stitching lines.

Cutting

From light tan prints & tonals:
- Cut 1 (1½") B square, and 1 each 1½" x 2½" C, 1½" x 3½" F and 1½" x 4½" G rectangles.

From dark tan prints & tonals:
- Cut 1 (1½") A square, and 1 each 1½" x 2½" D, 1½" x 3½" E, 1½" x 4½" H and 1½" x 5½" I rectangles.

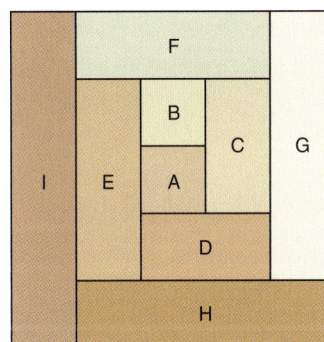

Log Cabin
5" x 5" Finished Block
Make 1

Completing the Pincushion
1. Sew the A and B squares together as shown in Figure 1; press. Working in a clockwise direction, stitch the C strip to the right and the D strip to the bottom, pressing after each seam.

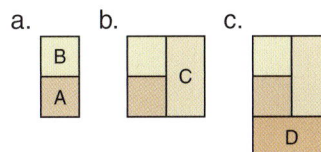

Figure 1

2. Continue adding E, F, G, H and I strips around clockwise, pressing after each addition, to complete the Log Cabin block.

3. Baste the batting square to the wrong side of the Log Cabin block and quilt by stitching in the ditch of the seams or as desired.

4. Prepare templates using the Comb, Tail Feathers and Beak patterns provided on the insert for this project.

5. Using the prepared templates, trace and cut two each combs and tail feathers from the red felt and two beaks from the gold felt.

6. Referring to Figure 2, position two combs together and, using two strands of matching floss, sew a blanket stitch around the edges. Repeat to make the tail feathers and beak.

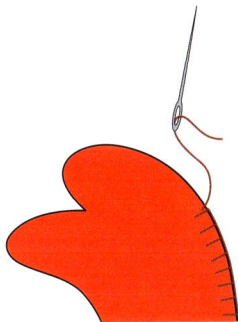

Figure 2

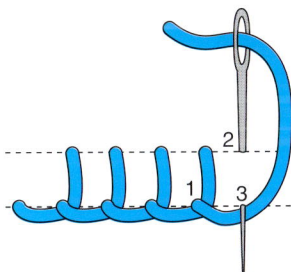

Blanket Stitch

Here's a Tip

A chicken made with a Log Cabin body would make a cute appliqué on a place mat or pot holder. Just use the patterns (enlarge them, if desired) to make fusible appliqués and make the body larger if needed by adding more rounds or by cutting the strips wider.

7. Matching raw edges, pin the felt pieces on the right side of the Log Cabin block with the beak ¾" down from the right top corner and the comb about 5⁄16" to the left of the same corner as shown in Figure 3. Pin the tail about 5⁄16" down from the top left corner. Machine-baste to secure.

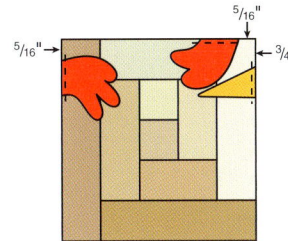

Figure 3

8. Pin the backing square right sides together to the right side of the block with all felt pieces between. Sew all around, leaving a 3" opening at the bottom. Trim the corners and turn right side out through the opening.

9. Fold the comb and beak out and position the black button for the eye in the upper right corner as shown on the Placement Diagram; sew in place.

10. Stuff the pincushion with fiberfill to a medium firmness.

11. Fold in the seam allowance on the opening and hand-sew the folded edges together to close. ●

Chicken Pincushion
Placement Diagram 5" x 5"

Come on a Safari With Me

This is a sturdy tote, practical and fun. The front features a pieced elephant bedecked in bright flowers with a big floppy ear.

Skill Level
Confident Beginner

Finished Size
Tote Size: 14" x 15" x 4"
Block Size: 17" x 17"
Number of Blocks: 1

Materials
- Small pieces green and gold batiks
- ½ yard gray-with-cream batik print
- ¾ yard cream-with-gray batik print
- ¾ yard red batik print
- 1¼ yards of 18"-wide foam stabilizer
- Batting scraps
- 3 (¾"-diameter) cover button kits
- 1 (⅞"-diameter) cream button
- Template material
- Thread
- Basic sewing tools and supplies

Project Notes
Read all instructions before beginning this project.

Stitch right sides together using a ¼" seam allowance unless otherwise specified.

Materials and cutting lists assume 40" of usable fabric width for yardage.

Refer to the project photo and Placement Diagram for positioning of pieces and stitching lines.

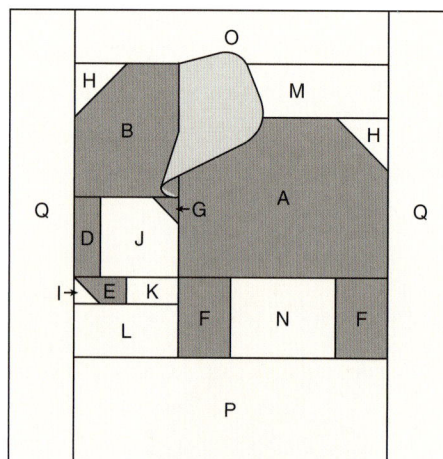

Elephant
18" x 17" Finished Block
Make 1

Cutting

From gray-with-cream batik:
- Cut 1 (4½" by fabric width) strip.
    Subcut strip into 2 (4½" x 14") T strips*
        and 1 (4½" x 5½") B rectangle.
- Cut 1 (6½" by fabric width) strip.
    Subcut strip into 1 (6½" x 8½") A rectangle.
- From remainder of strip, cut 1 (1½" by remaining fabric width) strip and 1 (2½" by remaining fabric width) strip.
    Subcut 1½"-wide strip into 1 each 1½" x 2½" C rectangle, 1½" x 3½" D rectangle and 1½" G square.
    Subcut 2½"-wide strip into 1 (1½" x 2½") E rectangle and 2 (2½" x 3½") F rectangles.

*If longer handles are preferred for a shoulder bag, measure and cut strips to desired length.

From cream-with-gray batik print:
- Cut 1 (17½" by fabric width) strip.
  Subcut strip into 1 (17½" x 18½") R rectangle and 2 (3½" x 17½") Q rectangles.
- From remainder of strip, cut 1 (12½" by remaining fabric width) strip and 1 (3½" by remaining fabric width) strip.
  Subcut 12½"-wide strip into 1 each 2½" x 12½" O strip and 4½" x 12½" P strip.
  Subcut 3½"-wide strip into 1 (3½") J square and 1 (3½" x 4½") N rectangle.
- Cut 1 (2½" by fabric width) strip.
  Subcut strip into 2 (2½") H squares, 1 each 1½" x 2½" K, 2½" x 4½" L and 2½" x 7½" M rectangle, and 2 (1½") I squares.

From red batik print:
- Cut 1 (17½" by fabric width) strip.
  Subcut strip into 2 (17½" x 18½") S rectangles.

From foam stabilizer:
- Cut 2 (18½" by fabric width) strips.
  Subcut strips into 2 (17½" x 18½") rectangles.
- Cut 4 (1½" x 14") handle strips. *If longer handles are cut, cut foam stabilizer to same length as fabric.

Completing the Block

1. Draw a diagonal line from corner to corner on the wrong side of each G, H and I square.

Sewing Tip

The stitch-and-flip method of adding a half triangle to a unit that will finish as a square or rectangle is a real time-saver, and it means you won't have to cut or sew a raw bias edge. It is important to note that, though many instructions tell you to stitch directly on the drawn diagonal line, it is important to stitch just slightly to the outside of that line. The drawn line is actually where you will fold the fabric over so if you stitch on it, it will be just shy of covering the corner. Stitch alongside the line and then open and press the seam flat before trimming the bottom layer.

2. Position an H square with right sides together on the top right corner of the A rectangle and stitch just inside the drawn line as shown in Figure 1. Trim seam to ¼" and press open to make an A-H unit.

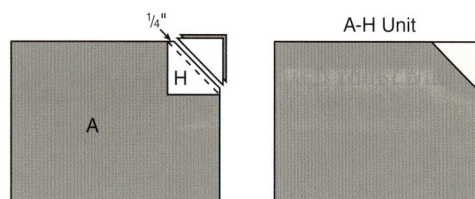

Figure 1

3. Referring to Figure 2, repeat step 2 stitching an I square to the C rectangle (Figure 2a) and an I square to the E rectangle (Figure 2b) to make a C-I and an E-I unit.

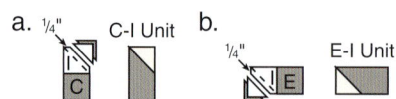

Figure 2

4. Repeat step 2, stitching the remaining H square to the upper left corner of the B rectangle to make a B-H unit as shown in Figure 3a. Stitch a G square to the upper right corner of the J square to make the G-J unit (Figure 3b).

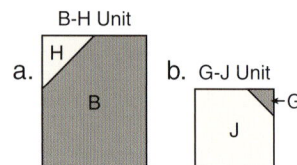

Figure 3

5. Referring to the block drawing for steps 5–10, sew the C-I unit to the left end of the M rectangle to make a C-I-M unit; press.

6. Arrange and stitch an F rectangle to opposite short sides of N to make an F-N unit; press.

7. Sew the C-I-M unit to the top of the A-H unit and the F-N unit to the bottom of the A-H unit to make the elephant body section; press.

8. Sew the D strip to the left edge of the G-J unit to make a D-G-J unit; press.

9. Sew the K rectangle to the right end of the E-I unit to make an E-I-K unit; press.

10. Arrange and vertically stitch the B-H unit, D-G-J unit, E-I-K unit and L rectangle together to make the elephant head section; press.

11. Prepare a template using the Ear pattern provided on the insert for this project. Trace the ear shape onto the wrong side of a scrap of the cream-with-gray batik print. Referring to Padded Appliqué on page 27, make one ear by layering the marked cream-with-gray batik print scrap right sides together with a gray-with-cream batik print scrap and batting scrap. Stitch, leaving long straight side open for turning. Trim seams, turn and press edges flat.

12. Pin the ear, cream side down, on the right side of the elephant head section, about 1" down from the top. Machine-baste in place as shown in Figure 4.

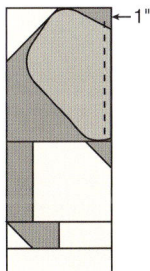

Figure 4

13. Referring to the block drawing, sew the elephant head and body sections together with the ear caught in the seam; press seam toward head section with ear flipped back toward the body section.

14. Sew the O strip to the top and the P strip to the bottom of the elephant; press. Sew Q strips to opposite sides to complete the Elephant block and tote front.

Preparing the Embellishments

1. Prepare templates using the Petal and Leaf patterns provided on the insert for this project.

2. Fold the remaining red batik print in half with right sides together; trace the petal shape 18 times on the top layer, leaving at least ¼" between shapes. Referring to Padded Appliqué on page 27, make 18 petals by layering the red print on a batting scrap. Stitch, leaving straight bottom edge open for turning. Trim seams, turn and press edges flat. If desired, hand quilt around each petal close to the edge.

3. Using a double strand of matching thread with a sturdy knot at the end, pick up one petal and make two or three gathering stitches across the bottom about ⅛" from the raw edge. Pull the thread to gather and then pick up a second petal and stitch across it as shown in Figure 5. Continue until you have six petals gathered on the thread. Insert the needle back into the first petal and pull thread to gather into a circle; knot and clip thread. Repeat to make a total of three flowers.

Figure 5

4. Following manufacturer's directions, complete three cover buttons with gold batik.

5. Fold the small piece of green batik in half with right sides together; trace the leaf shape four times on the top layer, leaving at least ¼" between shapes. Referring to Padded Appliqué on page 27, make four leaves by layering the green batik on a batting scrap. Stitch all around, cutting a slash for turning. Trim seams, turn, press edges flat and whipstitch opening closed.

Assembling the Tote

1. With right side up, layer and pin the tote front to one foam stabilizer rectangle, baste edges to secure. Repeat with the R rectangle and remaining stabilizer rectangle to make the tote back.

2. Quilt tote front by stitching in the ditch around the elephant patchwork. Quilt the back by stitching rows, a grid or as desired.

3. Arrange flowers and leaves on the Elephant block. Pin the leaves in place and remove the flowers. Attach leaves by stitching vein lines in each leaf, sewing through all layers.

4. To attach the flowers, use a double strand of strong thread with a sturdy knot at one end and insert the needle into the wrong side of the Elephant block, through the center opening of a flower. Go through the shank of a covered button and back down through the flower center as shown in Figure 6. Pull flower and button so they rest snugly on the surface, knot thread and clip. Repeat to attach the remaining flowers.

Figure 6

5. Sew the cream button to the elephant head for an eye.

6. If desired, referring to Figure 7, pleat the elephant ear to make it more dimensional. Fold ear forward at the bottom about ½" and hand-tack in place.

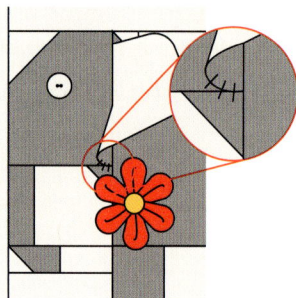

Figure 7

7. Pin the front and back tote sections right sides together and stitch a ¼" seam on the sides and bottom as shown in Figure 8a. Mark and cut 2" squares from both bottom corners of the tote (Figure 8b).

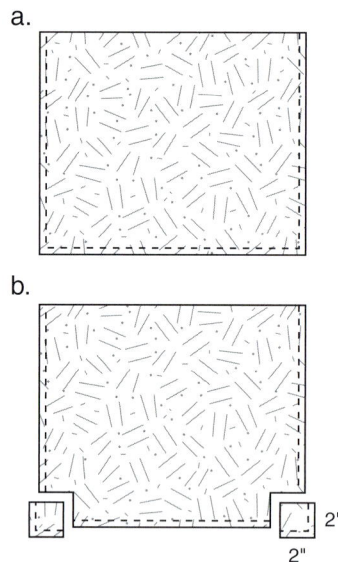

a.

b.

2"
2"

Figure 8

8. Referring to Figure 9, separate the front from the back at one of the cut corners and match the side and bottom seams; pin. Double-stitch ¼" from raw edges to form a box corner. Repeat for opposite corner. Turn the tote right side out.

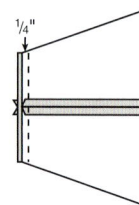

¼"

Figure 9

9. Press a ¼" hem on one long edge of each T strip.

10. Place a foam stabilizer handle strip in the center of the wrong side of T strip as shown in Figure 10. Fold up the side with the raw edge and fold down the side with the pressed edge. Topstitch ¼" from both long edges of the strip. Repeat to make a second handle.

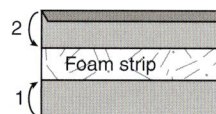

2

Foam strip

1

Figure 10

11. Referring to Figure 11, position the ends of a handle on the right side of the tote back, about 5" from the side seams with raw edges even; baste. Repeat with remaining handle on the tote front.

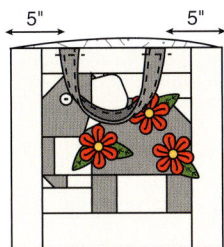

Figure 11

12. Repeat steps 7 and 8 using S rectangles to make the tote lining, leaving a 6" opening in the bottom seam. Do not turn right side out.

13. Place the tote inside the lining with right sides together, matching side seams. Stitch ¼" all around the top edge. Turn right side out through opening in bottom of lining, pushing the lining inside the tote and pulling the straps up. Fold in the seam allowance on the opening and hand-sew the folded edges together. Topstitch ¼" from the top edge to finish the tote. ●

Come on a Safari With Me
Placement Diagram 14" x 15" x 4"

Design Tip

This pieced Elephant block is large and would make a wonderful quilt block. Try making the elephants with big bright florals instead of adding dimensional flowers. The dimensional ear would still be a fun feature in an elephant quilt or you could eliminate that step.

Monkey See, Monkey Read

For many of us, glasses are a necessity! Having a cute quilted case to protect our glasses is practical and fun. And an extra benefit is that they are easier to find when you need them!

Skill Level
Beginner

Finished Size
Case Size: 4½" x 8", including binding

Materials
- Scraps tan and cream tonals
- ¼ yard dark pink tonal
- ⅓ yard light pink dot
- Batting scraps
- Dark brown all-purpose thread
- Dark brown embroidery floss
- Fusible web with paper release
- Template material
- Thread
- Basic sewing tools and supplies

Project Notes
Read all instructions before beginning this project.

Stitch right sides together using a ¼" seam allowance unless otherwise specified.

Materials and cutting lists assume 40" of usable fabric width for yardage.

Refer to the project photo and Placement Diagram for positioning of pieces and stitching lines.

Cutting

From dark pink tonal:
- Cut 1 (4½" by fabric width) strip.
  Subcut strip into 1 (4½" x 6½") A rectangle and 2 (4½" x 8") B rectangles.

From light pink dot:
- Cut 1 (2½" by fabric width) binding strip.
- Cut 1 (4½" by fabric width) strip.
  Subcut strip into 1 (4½" x 7¼") C rectangle.

From batting scraps:
- Cut 1 each 4½" x 8" and 4½" x 6½" rectangle.

Completing the Case

1. Baste the same-size batting rectangles to the wrong side of A and one B rectangle.

2. Prepare templates using the Body, Head, Snout, Ear and Tail patterns provided on the insert for this project.

3. Using the prepared templates, trace the shapes onto the paper side of fusible web, referring to information below for number to trace. Cut shapes apart and apply to wrong side of fabric as listed below:

- Tan tonal: 1 each body, head and tail; 2 ears
- Cream tonal: 1 snout

Here's a Tip

Monkey Wrench is a traditional quilt block that is fun to make and so versatile. This little monkey head would be a cute appliqué on the center square of a Monkey Wrench block! Enlarge it if you like and make enough blocks for a baby quilt!

4. Cut out shapes on traced lines and remove paper backing.

5. Center the body about 1" up from the bottom edge of the A pocket front. Add the head and snout and an ear on each side. Tuck the bottom of the tail under the side of the body as shown. Fuse in place.

6. Machine blanket-stitch all around the appliqués using matching thread.

7. Transfer the lines for the glasses and machine-stitch on the lines, using a short stitch and dark brown thread.

8. Make French knots for the two eyes on the head and two nostrils on the snout using two strands of dark brown floss.

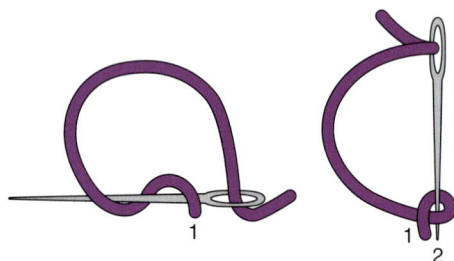

French Knot

9. Sew the C rectangle to the appliquéd pocket, right sides facing and matching the top raw edges as shown in Figure 1. Flip the C rectangle over to the wrong side of the pocket and match the sides and bottom edges, forming a narrow border of C at the top of A. Press and baste the edges together.

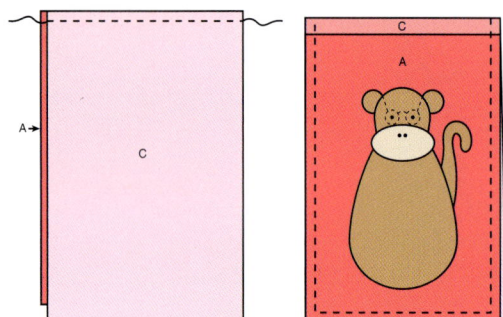

Figure 1

Here's a Tip

When sewing several layers together, you may find it easier to use binding clips, or even office-supply bulldog clips, to hold the layers together instead of pinning. They won't distort the edge as much and are easy to handle.

10. Quilt the pocket by stitching around the monkey appliqué or as desired. Stitch in the ditch of the A-C seam.

11. Layer the two B rectangles with wrong sides facing and the batting in between. Pin or baste to hold. Quilt a grid or as desired to finish the back of the case.

12. Pin the pocket to the quilted back, matching the bottom and side edges. Machine-baste to secure.

13. Prepare binding referring to Quilting Basics on page 61 and bind the edges to complete the case. ●

Monkey See, Monkey Read
Placement Diagram 4½" x 8",
including binding

Owl Needle Holder

This little owl needle holder opens his wings to reveal his stash of needles. He is lightly stuffed and can also be used as a pincushion.

Skill Level
Beginner

Finished Size
Approximately 3½" x 7" closed, including legs

Materials
- Small pieces brown tonal and black-with-dots
- Scraps cream and gold tonals or solids
- Small piece orange wool or acrylic felt
- Small piece batting
- 12" (⅜"-wide) brown grosgrain ribbon
- 2 (⁷⁄₁₆"-diameter) black buttons
- Cotton or polyester fiberfill
- Orange embroidery floss
- Fusible web with paper release
- Template material
- Thread
- Basic sewing tools and supplies

Project Notes
Read all instructions before beginning this project.

Stitch right sides together using a ¼" seam allowance unless otherwise specified.

Refer to the project photo and Placement Diagram for positioning of pieces and stitching lines.

Completing the Needle Holder
1. Prepare templates using the Body, Wing, Eyes, Beak, Tummy and Leg patterns provided on the insert for this project.

2. Use the prepared body template to trace and cut two bodies from the brown tonal for the front and back and one from the batting.

Here's a Tip
To cut shapes from felt, trace them onto the dull side of freezer paper, with a small margin between the shapes. Cut the shapes apart and iron the shiny side of the paper directly to the felt for about three seconds. The paper will stick and you can cut out the shape directly on the pattern lines. This method is very accurate and eliminates the need to make marks on the felt.

3. Baste the batting to the wrong side of the body front.

4. Using the prepared templates for eyes and beak, trace the shapes onto the paper side of fusible web, referring to information below for number to trace. Cut shapes apart and apply to the wrong side of the fabric as listed below:

- Cream: 1 eyes
- Gold: 1 beak

5. Cut out shapes on traced lines and remove paper backing.

6. Center the eyes and beak on the owl front, with the top of the eyes about ¾" down from the center top of the head and the beak slightly overlapping the eyes. Fuse in place.

7. Machine blanket-stitch around the appliqués using matching thread.

8. Using prepared templates, cut one tummy and four legs from orange felt.

9. Pin the tummy to the owl front just under the beak as shown in Figure 1. Use 2 strands of orange floss to hand blanket-stitch around the tummy.

Figure 1

Here's a Tip

You might like to enlarge this pattern to make a pillow! You can eliminate the ribbon and just leave the wings loose at the sides.

10. To make legs, place two legs together and hand-sew a blanket stitch around the edges using 2 strands of orange floss. Repeat for the second leg.

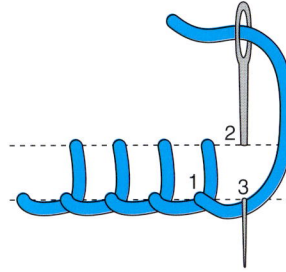

Blanket Stitch

11. Cut out four wings from black-with-dots. Cut the ribbon in half. Referring to Figure 2, place a length of ribbon on the right side of two wings, matching the ribbon end to the curved edge of the wing. Baste to hold.

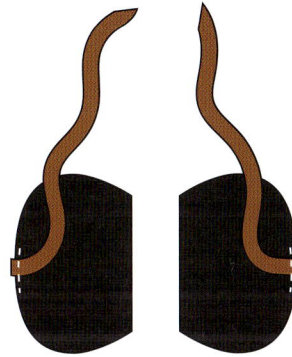

Figure 2

12. Place wings with ribbons right side up on a scrap of batting and loosely fold and pin the ribbon to keep it centered on the wing. Pin a second wing, right side down, to each. Stitch around the wing with a ¼" seam allowance, leaving open at the straight edge as shown in Figure 3. Cut out the batting to match the wing edge, clip the curves and turn the wings right side out through the open edge. Press the edges flat and topstitch close to the seam.

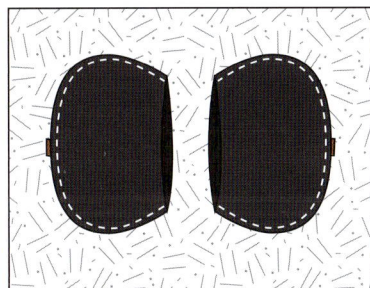

Figure 3

13. Referring to Figure 4, position the legs at the center bottom of the owl front, about ⅝" apart and pin a wing to each side; baste to secure. Cover the owl front body with the owl back body, right sides together, and stitch a ¼" seam all around, leaving a 2½" opening on one side. Clip curves and turn right side out through the opening, pulling the legs down and the wings out. Unpin the ribbon ends.

Figure 4

14. Stuff the shape lightly with fiberfill. Fold in the seam allowance on the opening and slip-stitch the folded edges together to close.

15. Sew the two black buttons to the cream eye area, sewing through to the back to slightly indent the eyes.

16. Store needles by slipping them through the tummy piece, and close the wings by tying the ribbon ends in a bow. ●

Owl Needle Holder
Placement Diagram
Approximately 3½" x 7" closed, including legs

Quilting Basics

The following is a reference guide. For more information, consult a comprehensive quilting book.

Always:

- Read through the entire pattern before you begin your project.
- Purchase quality, 100 percent cotton fabrics.
- When considering prewashing, do so with ALL of the fabrics being used. Generally, prewashing is not required in quilting.
- Use ¼" seam allowance for all stitching unless otherwise instructed.
- Use a short-to-medium stitch length.
- Make sure your seams are accurate.

Quilting Tools & Supplies

- Rotary cutter and mat
- Scissors for paper and fabric
- Non-slip quilting rulers
- Marking tools
- Sewing machine
- Sewing machine feet:
    - ¼" seaming foot (for piecing)
    - Walking or even-feed foot (for piecing or quilting)
    - Darning or free-motion foot (for free-motion quilting)
- Quilting hand-sewing needles
- Straight pins
- Curved safety pins for basting
- Seam ripper
- Iron and ironing surface

Basic Techniques

Appliqué

Fusible Appliqué

All templates are reversed for use with this technique.

1. Trace the instructed number of templates ¼" apart onto the paper side of paper-backed fusible web. Cut apart the templates, leaving a margin around each, and fuse to the wrong side of the fabric following fusible web manufacturer's instructions.

2. Cut the appliqué pieces out on the traced lines, remove paper backing and fuse to the background referring to the appliqué motif given.

3. Finish appliqué raw edges with a straight, satin, blanket, zigzag or blind-hem machine stitch with matching or invisible thread.

Turned-Edge Appliqué

1. Trace the printed reversed templates onto template plastic. Flip the template over and mark as the right side.

2. Position the template, right side up, on the right side of fabric and lightly trace, spacing images ½" apart. Cut apart, leaving a ¼" margin around the traced lines.

3. Clip curves and press edges ¼" to the wrong side around the appliqué shape.

4. Referring to the appliqué motif, pin or baste appliqué shapes to the background.

5. Hand-stitch shapes in place using a blind stitch and thread to match or machine-stitch using a short blind hemstitch and either matching or invisible thread.

Borders

Most patterns give an exact size to cut borders. You may check those sizes by comparing them to the horizontal and vertical center measurements of your quilt top.

Straight Borders

1. Mark the centers of the side borders and quilt top sides.

2. Stitch borders to quilt top sides with right sides together and matching raw edges and center marks using a ¼" seam. Press seams toward borders.

3. Repeat with top and bottom border lengths.

Mitered Borders

1. Add at least twice the border width to the border lengths instructed to cut.

2. Center and sew the side borders to the quilt, beginning and ending stitching ¼" from the quilt corner and backstitching (Figure 1). Repeat with the top and bottom borders.

Figure 1

3. Fold and pin quilt right sides together at a 45-degree angle on one corner (Figure 2). Place a straightedge along the fold and lightly mark a line across the border ends.

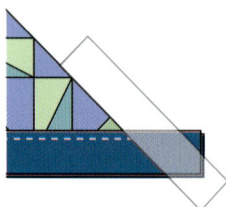

Figure 2

4. Stitch along the line, backstitching to secure. Trim seam to ¼" and press open (Figure 3).

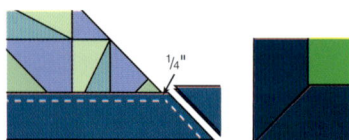

Figure 3

Quilt Backing & Batting

We suggest that you cut your backing and batting 8" larger than the finished quilt-top size. If preparing the backing from standard-width fabrics, remove the selvages and sew two or three lengths together; press seams open. If using 108"-wide fabric, trim to size on the straight grain of the fabric.

Prepare batting the same size as your backing. You can purchase prepackaged sizes or battings by the yard and trim to size.

Quilting

1. Press quilt top on both sides and trim all loose threads.

2. Make a quilt sandwich by layering the backing right side down, batting and quilt top centered right side up on flat surface and smooth out. Pin or baste layers together to hold.

3. Mark quilting design on quilt top and quilt as desired by hand or machine. *Note: If you are sending your quilt to a professional quilter, contact them for specifics about preparing your quilt for quilting.*

4. When quilting is complete, remove pins or basting. Trim batting and backing edges even with raw edges of quilt top.

Binding the Quilt

1. Join binding strips on short ends with diagonal seams to make one long strip; trim seams to ¼" and press seams open (Figure 4).

2. Fold 1" of one short end to wrong side and press. Fold the binding strip in half with wrong sides together along length, again referring to Figure 4; press.

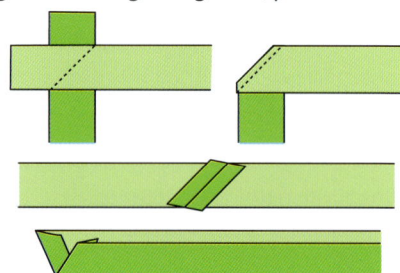

Figure 4

3. Starting about 3" from the folded short end, sew binding to quilt top edges, matching raw edges and using a ¼" seam. Stop stitching ¼" from corner and backstitch (Figure 5).

Figure 5

4. Fold binding up at a 45-degree angle to seam and then down even with quilt edges, forming a pleat at corner, referring to Figure 6.

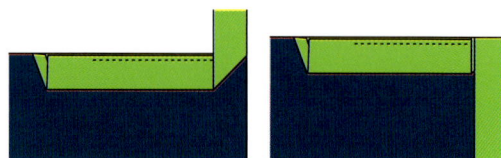

Figure 6

5. Resume stitching from corner edge as shown in Figure 6, down quilt side, backstitching ¼" from next corner. Repeat, mitering all corners, stitching to within 3" of starting point.

6. Trim binding end long enough to tuck inside starting end and complete stitching (Figure 7).

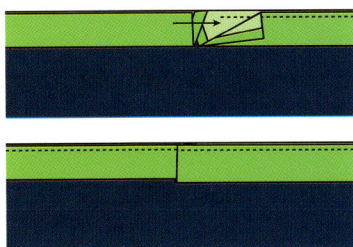

Figure 7

7. Fold binding to quilt back and stitch in place by hand or machine to complete your quilt.

Quilting Terms

- **Appliqué:** Adding fabric motifs to a foundation fabric by hand or machine (see Appliqué section of Basic Techniques).
- **Basting:** This temporarily secures layers of quilting materials together with safety pins, thread or a spray adhesive in preparation for quilting the layers.

  Use a long, straight stitch to hand- or machine-stitch one element to another holding the elements in place during construction and usually removed after construction.
- **Batting:** An insulating material made in a variety of fiber contents that is used between the quilt top and back to provide extra warmth and loft.
- **Binding:** A finishing strip of fabric sewn to the outer raw edges of a quilt to cover them.

  Straight-grain binding strips, cut on the crosswise straight grain of the fabric (see Straight & Bias Grain Lines illustration), are commonly used.

  Bias binding strips are cut at a 45-degree angle to the straight grain of the fabric. They are used when binding is being added to curved edges.
- **Block:** The basic quilting unit that is repeated to complete the quilt's design composition. Blocks can be pieced, appliquéd or solid and are usually square or rectangular in shape.
- **Border:** The frame of a quilt's central design used to visually complete the design and give the eye a place to rest.
- **Fabric Grain:** The fibers that run either parallel (lengthwise grain) or perpendicular (crosswise grain) to the fabric selvage are straight grain.

Bias is any diagonal line between the lengthwise or crosswise grain. At these angles the fabric is less stable and stretches easily. The true bias of a woven fabric is a 45-degree angle between the lengthwise and crosswise grain lines.

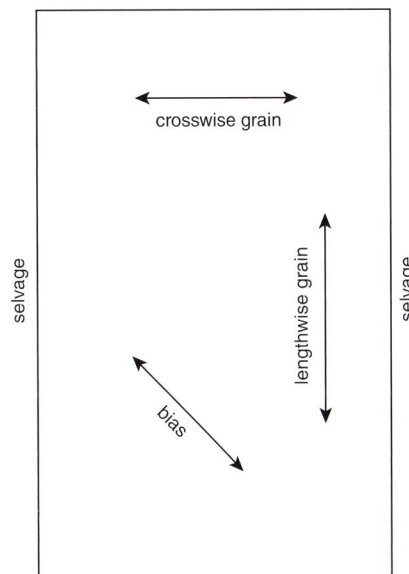

Straight & Bias Grain Lines

- **Mitered Corners:** Matching borders or turning bindings at a 45-degree angle at corners.
- **Patchwork:** A general term for the completed blocks or quilts that are made from smaller shapes sewn together.
- **Pattern:** This may refer to the design of a fabric or to the written instructions for a particular quilt design.
- **Piecing:** The act of sewing smaller pieces and/or units of a block or quilt together.

  Paper or foundation piecing is sewing fabric to a paper or cloth foundation in a certain order.

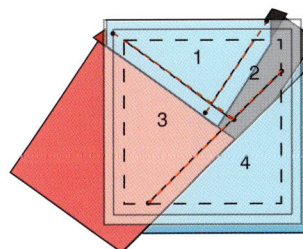

Foundation Piecing

String or chain piecing is sewing pieces together in a continuous string without clipping threads between sections.

String or Chain Piecing

- **Pressing:** Pressing is the process of placing the iron on the fabric, lifting it off the fabric and placing it down in another location to flatten seams or crease fabric without sliding the iron across the fabric.

  Quilters do not usually use steam when pressing, since it can easily distort fabric shapes.

  Generally, seam allowances are pressed toward the darker fabric in quilting so that they do not show through the lighter fabric.

  Seams are pressed in opposite directions where seams are being joined to allow seams to butt against each other and to distribute bulk.

  Seams are pressed open when multiple seams come together in one place.

  If you have a question about pressing direction, consult a comprehensive quilting guide for guidance.
- **Quilt (noun):** A sandwich of two layers of fabric with a third insulating material between them that is then stitched together with the edges covered or bound.
- **Quilt (verb):** Stitching several layers of fabric materials together with a decorative design. Stippling, crosshatch, channel, in-the-ditch, free-motion, allover and meandering are all terms for quilting designs.

- **Quilt Sandwich:** A layer of insulating material between a quilt's top and back fabric.
- **Rotary Cutting:** Using a rotary cutting blade and straightedge to cut fabric.
- **Sashing:** Strips of fabric sewn between blocks to separate or set off the designs.
- **Subcut:** A second cutting of rotary-cut strips that makes the basic shapes used in block and quilt construction.
- **Template:** A pattern made from a sturdy material which is then used to cut shapes for patchwork and appliqué quilting.

Quilting Skill Levels

- **Beginner:** A quilter who has been introduced to the basics of cutting, piecing and assembling a quilt top and is working to master these skills. Someone who has the knowledge of how to sandwich, quilt and bind a quilt, but may not have necessarily accomplished the task yet.

- **Confident Beginner:** A quilter who has pieced and assembled several quilt tops and is comfortable with the process, and is now ready to move on to more challenging techniques and projects using at least two different techniques.

- **Intermediate:** A quilter who is comfortable with most quilting techniques and has a good understanding for design, color and the whole process. A quilter who is experienced in paper piecing, bias piecing and projects involving multiple techniques. Someone who is confident in making fabric selections other than those listed in the pattern.

- **Advanced:** A quilter who is looking for a challenging design. Someone who knows she or he can make any type of quilt. Someone who has the skills to read, comprehend and complete a pattern, and is willing to take on any technique. A quilter who is comfortable in her or his skills and has the ability to select fabric suited to the project. ●

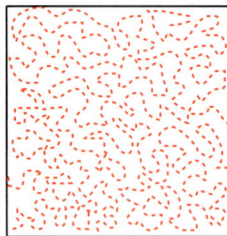

Meandering

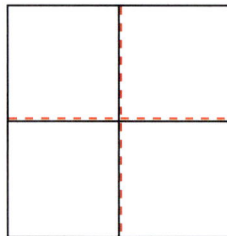

Stitch-in-the-ditch

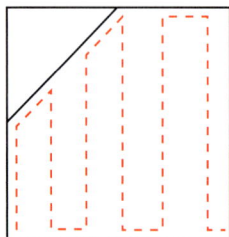

Channel

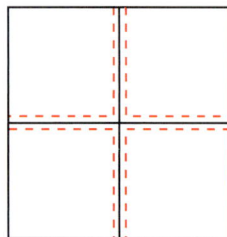

Outline

Annie's® Published by Annie's, 306 East Parr Road, Berne, IN 46711. Printed in USA. Copyright © 2018 Annie's. All rights reserved. This publication may not be reproduced in part or in whole without written permission from the publisher.

RETAIL STORES: If you would like to carry this publication or any other Annie's publications, visit AnniesWSL.com.

Every effort has been made to ensure that the instructions in this publication are complete and accurate. We cannot, however, take responsibility for human error, typographical mistakes or variations in individual work. Please visit AnniesCustomerService.com to check for pattern updates.

ISBN: 978-1-59012-930-2

1 2 3 4 5 6 7 8 9